THOMAS AQUINAS
& THE LITURGY

THOMAS AQUINAS
& THE LITURGY

David Berger

Sapientia Press
of Ave Maria University

Sanctae dei genitrici
sedi sapientiae

In signum gratitudinis
et filialis obedientiae

Requests for permission to make copies of any part of the work should be directed to:

Sapientia Press
of Ave Maria University
24 Frank Lloyd Wright Drive
Ann Arbor, MI 48106
888-343-8607

Cover image: Fra Angelico (1387–1455), Madonna of the Shadows. Museo de S. Marco, Florence

Photo credit: Scala/Art Resource, NY

Cover design: Eloise Anagnost

Printed in the United States of America.

Library of Congress Control Number: 2004090918

ISBN 0-9706106-8-8

Table of Contents

Preface

THIS LITTLE BOOK has to be prefaced by a few brief acknowledgments. The first one is directed to Rome, to His Eminence Alfons M. Cardinal Stickler, S.D.B. Despite an arduous period of convalescence, he read the manuscript of the first German edition with "lively interest" and encouraged me to have the book published immediately. In this context particularly grateful mention is also due to the kind reviews, in many cases very extensive, by Professor Walter Hoeres in the *Tagespost*, Monsignore Professor Dr. Brunero Gherardini (Vatican) in *Divinitas*, Jens Mersch in the *Kirchliche Umschau*, Raphael Delavigne in *Catholica*, Monsignore Ulrich-Paul Lange in *Theologisches*, Professor Manfred Hauke in the *Rivista Teologica di Lugano*, Fr. Aidan Nichols in *The Thomist*, Fr. Antolin González Fuente in *Angelicum*, and Fr. Tadeus Guz in *Doctor Angelicus*. We now have a translation of this little work into English to stand beside the French publication that is already in its second edition. This fact delights the author all the more as he thinks he can detect a certain budding and hopeful

Thomist renaissance in the English-speaking countries, which might even come to influence the home country of the Reformation where Thomism still has a hard time of it. A last word of thanks goes therefore to Sapientia Press and its associate editor, Matthew Levering, a fellow Thomist theologian, as well as to the translator, Christopher Grosz, who took it upon himself to translate the German original into English.

CHAPTER 1

Why Thomas Aquinas in Particular?

D EALING WITH the fundamentals of liturgiology, addressing the question of what liturgy is, in a real and authentic sense, requires no separate justification. Following decades of often ill-advised reforms and experiments with the liturgy that mostly cast aside all tradition, many different voices have been raised calling for a "start from within," a "rediscovery of the living center," a "penetration into the inner fabric of the liturgy," which then might be able to offer the measure for what is permissible and/or required in the liturgy.[1]

Yet, why should Thomas Aquinas of all theologians have anything to say to us today? Someone who died more than seven hundred years ago and whose questions— given the changed context in which he thought and wrote—obviously must have been quite different from those we ask ourselves today? A saint whom the history of

---

[1] Joseph Cardinal Ratzinger, "Zum Gedenken an Klaus Gamber," in Wilhelm Nyssen, ed., *Simandron. Der Wachklopfer. Gedenkschrift für Klaus Gamber* (Cologne: Luthe-Verlag, 1989), 13. Cf. statements by Alfons M. Cardinal Stickler: ibid., 17–19.

theology rightly considers the most important representative of scholasticism, that is, the kind of theology which
many a liturgical scholar considers the theoretical correlate
to the presumed decline of liturgy that allegedly started in
the Middle Ages through rationalism, legalism, and an
exaggerated leaning toward the Church of Rome?[2] A theologian who in his explanation of the liturgy of Holy Mass
still employed the controversial concepts of allegory and
rememoratio (cf. chapter IV)? A thinker, above all, of
whom one of the best-known German-speaking experts
says: "Thomas had . . . obviously no great sense for
liturgy," and declaring a few pages later that "[i]n Thomas'
Order, the Order of Preachers, the celebration of the
liturgy—the divine office and the celebration of the
Eucharist—is a central element of monastic life . . . [and
yet] Thomas has no sense for that?"[3] The following treatise
seeks to give an answer to such questions.[4]

---

[2] Following A. Jungmann, this thesis is advocated by Marcel
Metzger, *Geschichte der Liturgie* (Paderborn: Schöningh, 1998),
127–44; and Geoffrey Hull, *The Banished Heart. Origins of
Heteropraxis in the Catholic Church* (Richmond: Spes Nova
League, 1995). On Hull cf. Helmut Rückriegel, "Papsttum,
Gehorsam—und der liturgische Traditionsbruch," *Una Voce
Korrespondenz* 26 (1996): 391–415. Closely connected is the
thesis, first advocated in Germany by Theodor Klauser, of the
fossilization of the Roman liturgy from the twelfth century
until the liturgical reform. Today however this thesis is considered "generally refuted." Benedikt Kranemann, "Liturgiewissenschaft angesichts der Zeitenwende," in Hubert Wolf,
ed., *Die katholisch-theologischen Disziplinen in Deutschland
1870–1962* (Paderborn: Schöningh, 1999), 365.

[3] Otto H. Pesch, *Thomas von Aquin. Größe und Grenze mittelalterlicher Theologie* (Mainz: Gründewald, 1995), 76, 346.

[4] Though no comprehensive work of our theme exists in German, there are a number of treatises in other languages:

The Authority of St. Thomas

From a purely formal aspect, it is only logical first to examine the central questions of theology in light of Aquinas, given the preeminent authority over all other theologians which the Church's teaching office and especially the popes of the last centuries have accorded him. "Councils and Popes competed in their tribute to the great Thomas Aquinas. Which of the two highest ecclesial authorities has done more to promote his fame, we cannot say. Their synergy was in any case causally reciprocal."[5] We will restrict ourselves here to citing only a few of the most important and impressive of these statements.[6]

Pope John XXII remarked at the canonization of Aquinas in the year 1323 that Thomas had illuminated the Church more than all other teachers of holy theology[7] and accorded him, as the first of the newer theologians, a place alongside the four great Fathers of the ancient Church.

J. Menessier, "L'idée du sacré et le cult d'aprés S. Thomas," *RSPT* 19 (1930): 63–82; Jean-Michel Hanssens, "De natura liturgiae ad mentem S. Thomae," *PRMCL* 24 (1935): 127–65; Joseph Lécuyer, "Reflexions sur la théologie du cult selon saint Thomas," *RT* 55 (1955): 339–62; Liam G. Walsh, "Liturgy in the Theology of St. Thomas," *Thomist* 38 (1974): 557–83; Antolin González Fuente, "La theologia nella liturgia e la liturgia nella teologia in san Tommaso d'Aquino," *Angelicum* 74 (1997): 359–417, 551–601.

[5] Gallus M. Manser, *Das Wesen des Thomismus* (Freiburg/Switzerland: Paulusverlag, 1949), 79.

[6] Cf. Joachim-Joseph Berthier, *Sanctus Thomas Aquinas "Doctor Communis" Ecclesiae, Vol. I: Testimonia Ecclesiae,* (Rome: Typographia Editrice Nazionale, 1914); Jacobo Maria Ramirez, *De auctoritate doctrinali S. Thomae Aquinatis* (Salamanca: Sanctum Stephanum, 1952).

[7] "Ipse plus illuminavit ecclesiam, quam omnes alii doctores."

Another important stage in the elevation of the Doctor Angelicus[8] was the Council of Trent (1545–1563). Cesare Baronius, the famous historian of this council, notes in this context that St. Thomas's decisive influence on the Council Fathers is almost beyond expression.[9] Pope Leo XIII in his Encyclical *Aeterni Patris* recalls the fact that St. Thomas's *Summa theologiae*, together with the Holy Scripture and the books containing the papal decrees, lay open on the council table during the entire Tridentinum and was assiduously consulted by the Council Fathers.[10] Thus on a question of profoundest importance for the liturgy—that of the real presence—the Council referred almost literally to a text by St. Thomas from the *Summa theologiae* (III, q. 75, a. 4).[11]

This indicates that the teaching of St. Thomas was considered to be a light of orthodoxy and a shield against heterodoxy. But this is demonstrated particularly emphatically in the second half of the nineteenth and the first

---

[8] Concerning the title, see Ferdinand Holböck, "Thomas von Aquin als 'Doctor Angelicus'," *Studi tomistici* 2 (1977): 199–217.

[9] Berthier, *Sanctus Thomas,* 402: "Vix quisquam ennarare sufficiat, quot vir sanctissimus atque eruditissimus Theologorum praeconiis celebretur, quantumque illius illibatae doctrinae a sanctis Patribus in sacrosancto oecumenico concilio considentibus fuerit acclamatus."

[10] Ibid., 212: "Sed haec est maxima et Thomae propria, nec cum quopiam ex doctoribus catholicis communicata laus, quod patres Tridentini . . . una cum divinae Scripturae codicibus et Pontificum Maximorum decretis, Summam Thomae Aquinatis super altari patere voluerunt, unde consilium, rationes, oracula peterentur."

[11] Cf. Antonio Piolanti, *Il Mistero Eucaristico* (Città del Vaticano: Liberia Editrice Vaticana, 1983), 249.

half of the twentieth century. In addition to the many addresses made by the popes and the XXIV Thomist theses of the Pontifical Congregation of Studies (DH 3601–3624), special mention must be made of the encyclical letters *Aeterni Patris* (1879) by Leo XIII, *Studiorum Ducem* (1923) by Pius XI, and *Humani Generis* (1950) by Pius XII, as well as the many clear and far-sighted statements made by Pope St. Pius X in the context of combating the heresy of Modernism. Pius X identifies the core evil of the various strands of Modernism, which he and his successors so courageously confronted and which to this day are still virulent in modified versions,[12] in the statement of the encyclical *Pascendi*: "Further let Professors remember that they cannot set St. Thomas aside, especially in metaphysical questions, without grave detriment."[13] Supplementing this is Pius XI in his *Studiorum Ducem*: "It is therefore clear why modernists are so amply justified in fearing no doctor of the Church so much as Thomas Aquinas."[14]

At the Second Vatican Council Cardinal Bacci was thus able to note: "Wishing to dispute the pre-eminence

---

[12] Cf. William J. Hoye, *Gotteserfahrung?* (Zürich: Benziger, 1993), 33–34: "Modernism, condemned in 1907, exerts nevertheless an influence of present day theology which can hardly be overestimated. . . . Everything else is relativized from this perspective [of subjectivism]."

[13] "Aquinatem deserere . . . non sine magno detrimento esse!" Cf. similarly his address to the professors of the Pontifical Academy of St. Thomas in 1914: "Nimirum curae habeant a via et ratione Aquinatis numquam discedere" (Berthier, *Sanctus Thomas,* 368).

[14] Quoted from Anton Rohrbasser, ed., *Heilslehre der Kirche* (Freiburg/Switzerland: Paulusverlag, 1953), No. 1945.

of Thomas Aquinas would mean placing the Council above and against the Popes, who have offered more than eighty statements on this subject."[15] It thus does not come as a surprise that Vatican II expressly underscores the authority of St. Thomas in two documents. *Optatam Totius* makes stipulations for the training of theologians: "In order that they may illumine the mysteries of salvation as completely as possible, the students should learn to penetrate them more deeply with the help of speculation, under the guidance of St. Thomas, and to perceive their interconnections."[16] The *Declaratio* concerning Christian education in its turn presents St. Thomas as the illuminating role model for all universities and faculties under the jurisdiction of the Church regarding the synthesis of faith and reason in the one truth—which is the fundamental theological question.[17]

If one also considers that Vatican II is the first ecumenical council in Church history that "expressly mentions one individual author by his name,"[18] the importance that the Church's teaching office still accords to St. Thomas becomes sufficiently clear. Wholly within this understanding, Pope John Paul II emphasized in his

---

[15] Quoted from Holböck, "Thomas von Aquin," 199.

[16] Latin *mysteria*. The closeness of the term *mysterium* with the object and concept of the term *sacramentum*, and hence with liturgy, at least suggests the special role of St. Thomas in liturgical questions!

[17] *Optatam Totius* 16; *Gravissimum educationis* 10. Cf. CIC 252 § 3.

[18] Josef Pieper, "Über einen verschollenen Vorschlag zum Zweiten Vatikanum," in Walter Baier et al., eds., *Weisheit Gottes—Weisheit der Welt. Festschrift für Cardinal Ratzinger,* Vol. II (St. Ottilien: Eosverlag, 1987), 971–75.

landmark encyclical *Fides et Ratio* (1998) that "the Church has been justified in consistently proposing St. Thomas as a master of thought and a model of the right way to do theology" (No. 43). He goes on to quote *Aeterni Patris*: "his thought scales 'heights unthinkable to human intelligence'" (No. 44).

Is Thomas Still Up-to-Date?[19]

This unequivocal and preeminent authority accorded to St. Thomas contrasts sharply with the unprecedented collapse Thomism has suffered since the middle of the nineteen-sixties, from which it is only gradually beginning to recover.[20] What caused the collapse that brought a seven-hundred-year-old tradition to the edge of complete disintegration? To be sure, to answer this question fully one would have to consider many factors external to Thomism. But Neo-Thomism, which on the eve of that collapse dominated philosophical and theological work undertaken within an ecclesial context, seems to have played a part in it also. Greatly influenced by the Jesuits (Joseph Maréchal, Karl Rahner, Johannes B. Metz,

---

[19] Cf. David Berger, *Thomismus. Große Leitmotive der thomistischen Synthese und ihre Aktualität für die Gegenwart* (Cologne: Editiones thomisticae, 2001).

[20] Pope John Paul II, in *Crossing the Threshold of Hope,* trans. Jenny and Martha McPhee (New York: Random House, 1994), notes that "today, unfortunately, the *Summa Theologica* has been somewhat neglected" (p. 29). Thomas F. O'Meara, OP, remarks in *Thomas Aquinas Theologian* (Notre Dame: University of Notre Dame Press, 1997), 198: "The effect of the Second Vatican Council upon Thomism, however, seemed to be a disaster. . . . Aquinas' influence was reduced, as contemporary or biblical theologies replaced neo-scholasticism."

Bernard Lonergan) and characterized by a standpoint based on transcendental philosophy, it was primarily concerned with a conclusive and smooth presentation of Thomas's topicality in the light of modern philosophy and theology. This resulted however in the difference between Thomas and modernity being smoothed out in a manner that showed little sensitivity for historical contexts, so that the specific character of the Thomist synthesis—and hence its critical potential—was suppressed.[21]

This problem is particularly pronounced in the reception of Thomas by J. B. Metz and his teacher Karl Rahner. In both his *Theological Investigations* and in a preface to Metz's doctoral thesis, Karl Rahner states: "Any restoration of the former seminary Thomism, or of a direct and almost naïve commitment to Thomas as to a contemporary figure, would be a betrayal of the Church and the men of today."[22] All we are left with is this: "A Thomas, who stands at the beginning of the time which is still ours today . . . can still be our teacher today . . . can be a man, who—with others—constitutes the still half hidden beginning of that time, which is still our time: the modern age."[23]

Quite apart from the fact that Rahner strikes the wrong note in the first passage quoted above, the upshot of a Thomism updated in such a fashion is obvious. What would be more boring than a Thomas who was required only to vote in favor of our preconceived opinion, who

21 John I. Jenkins, *Knowledge and Faith in Thomas Aquinas* (Cambridge: Cambridge University Press, 1997), 2–3, 101–28.

22 Karl Rahner, *Theological Investigations,* Vol. XIII, trans. David Bourke (New York: Crossroad, 1975), 4

23 Johann B. Metz, *Christliche Anthropozentrik. Über die Denkform des Thomas von Aquin* (Munich: Kösel, 1962), 19.

merely conveyed to us, albeit in a naïve form, what we already knew in complete and finalized form? Would not the only consequence then be finally to bid farewell to a Thomism which basically constituted nothing more than an underdeveloped mode of modern thinking and hence was incapable of offering a true alternative?

Does this problematic situation not bring us to giving up completely the search for a topicality for St. Thomas in the present age, if we do not wish to fall victim to a hopeless anachronism? No. That an answer is required follows precisely from this context. This context demonstrates that a specifically structured updating of Thomism has failed. It has enriched theology, but in many aspects, it has heavily burdened it. This, together with the lasting question of what service Thomism can do at the present hour to theology and the Church—which is explicitly demanding that very service[24]—is the background that guides our study.

Indeed, as other scholars have implied,[25] the present-day topicality of Thomism does not reveal itself in those studies in which Thomas is simply made contemporaneous with the dogmas of our own present time, regardless of whether we call it the modern age, modernity, postmodernity, or something else. The contemporaneity sought here is rather that of the non-contemporaneous.[26]

---

[24] Cf. Hans C. Schmidbaur, *Personarum Trinitas. Die trinitarische Gotteslehre des hl. Thomas von Aquin* (St. Ottilien: Eosverlag, 1995), 17.

[25] Ibid., 15–17; Pesch, *Thomas von Aquin,* 40–41; Jenkins, *Knowledge and Faith,* 3; Gion Darms, *700 Jahre Thomas von Aquin* (Freiburg/Switzerland: Paulusverlag, 1974), passim.

[26] Cf. Leo Scheffczyk, "Theologie und Moderne," *Forum Katholische Theologie* 13 (1997): 283–90.

The real topicality of Thomism reveals itself in its other-
ness: where it breaks through those superficial plausibili-
ties that support the spirit of the age's articles of faith and
which have penetrated deep into today's ecclesial parl-
ance—right into the liturgy—creating their own language
along the way; where its timeless wisdom causes us a
painful yet salutary disquiet, breaks open the narrow confines of our thinking, drags us out of our own house of
temporality in order to guide us to a "progress independent of and above all time, all changing styles of question-
ing and all theological epochs."[27]

What the philosopher Hermann Kleber remarked in a
similar context holds equally true for the topicality claimed
for Thomism: "Faced with the great general human questions that concern all human beings in all epochs and cul-
tures, every epoch and every culture has its own specific
blind spots and hardened prejudices. These have generally
been neither consciously nor deliberately fostered, but are
the result of convictions, opinions, judgments and concepts that are accepted without reflection. Serious engage-
ment with a historically earlier position therefore offers
the opportunity to liberate oneself from the bias of prejudices and unjustified convictions of one's own epoch and
culture, to understand one's own position better, to rela-
tivize and . . . *if need be to correct it.*"[28]

---

27 Schmidbaur, *Personarum Trinitas,* 17.

28 Hermann Kleber, *Glück als Lebensziel. Untersuchungen zur
Philosophie des Glücks bei Thomas von Aquin* (Munster: Aschendorff, 1988), 7.

CHAPTER 2

The Liturgy in the Life
of the Doctor Angelicus

I T WAS A PATRIARCH of Constantinople, the learned
Cardinal Bessarion—a participant at the Council of
Florence (1439)—who said about the "last great teacher of
a then still undivided Christendom" (as Pieper has put it)
that as Thomas was "the most learned among the saints so
he was simultaneously the holiest among the learned":
"non minus inter sanctos doctissimus, quam inter doctos
sanctissimus." [1] Cardinal Bessarion put into a concise statement what modern literature has too often forgotten about
Aquinas: His philosophical–theological synthesis is born
out of the effulgence of his holiness and becomes truly visible to later generations only in this effulgence. The attention of Thomas's interpreters hence ought to focus as
much on the classical as on the modern-day research into
the spirituality which Thomas lived and taught. [2] Such an

---

[1] Berthier, *Sanctus Thomas*, 679. On the influence of St.
Thomas on the Greek Orthodox Church, see Romanus Cessario, *Le Thomisme et les Thomistes* (Paris: Cerf, 1999), 75–76.

[2] Cf. Réginald Garrigou-Lagrange, *Christian Perfection and Con-
templation* (St. Louis: B. Herder, 1939); Magnus Beck, *Wege der
Mystik bei Thomas von Aquin* (St. Ottilien: Eosverlag, 1990);
Marie-Dominique Philippe, *Saint Thomas docteur témoin de*

approach to Thomas's work is also justified from a theoretical scientific view. In the historiography of philosophy, the life and the teaching of a thinker are now generally considered in their reciprocal dependence.[3]

This applies a fortiori to the sphere of liturgy, for in no other sphere is the sacred science (research into the *lex credendi*) so closely linked to faith as, in celebratory performance, it is here.[4]

What role then does the liturgy play in the life of St. Thomas Aquinas?

The Liturgical Spirituality of the Sons of St. Benedict of Nursia

The human being that the postconciliar reformed liturgy (as it de facto generally takes shape) seems to produce is hardly one who contemplates and receives. Rather, the actively doing person, someone who thinks he is the

---

Jésus (Fribourg: Paulusverlag, 1992); Jean-Pierre Torrell, *Saint Thomas d'Aquin, maître spirituel* (Fribourg: Editions Universitaires de Fribourg, 1996); my review of this in *Forum Katholische Theologie* 14 (1998): 69–71; David Berger, "Thomas von Aquin—Lehrer der Spiritualität," *Der Fels* 30 (1999): 12–15.

3 Cf. Rudi Imbach, "Interesse am Mittelalter. Beobachtungen zur Historiographie der mittelalterlichen Philosophie," *Theologische Quartalschrift* 172 (1992): 196–207. In my book, *Thomas von Aquin begegnen* (Augsburg: Sankt Ulrich Verlag, 2002), I tried to provide an introduction to the life and work of Aquinas by using this method.

4 This is demonstrated in the reciprocal causality of *lex credendi* and *lex orandi*! On this see Alfons M. Cardinal Stickler, "Der Vorrang des Göttlichen in der Liturgie," *Una Voce Korrespondenz* 27 (1997): 323.

active shaper of liturgy, seems to be promoted. To quote
Cardinal Ratzinger's oft-expressed criticism, however,
such a person underestimates grace-given contemplation
in favor of an "active doing . . . the shallow product of
the moment."[5] In the life of St. Thomas, we encounter
the light of an altogether different understanding of
human nature. Almost all biographies present Thomas as
a "homo magnae contemplationis et orationis" ("a man
wholly assigned to contemplation and prayer").[6]

Indeed, classical liturgy calls for and shapes such a person, devoted to contemplation, capable of receiving, humble,[7] not pelagian,[8] who can above all look wholly away
from himself and open himself to one who is greater
and other. Such a person recognizes that the liturgy, as
Romano Guardini reminded us, has something in common with the stars: "with their eternally fixed and even
course, their unchangeable order, their profound silence,
and the infinite space in which they are poised."[9] St.
Thomas seems to have been endowed with this contem-
plative spirit from very early on. He grew up amongst the
Benedictines of Monte Cassino, where he was educated in
the spirit of St. Benedict of Nursia, in whose order the
liturgy holds pride of place both in its importance and in

---

[5] Ratzinger, *Klaus Gamber,* 14–15.

[6] Neapoli, 77.

[7] Aquinas's biographers all keep stressing this character trait.

[8] St. Thomas's teachings on grace, especially in their final ver-
sion, are, together with the writings of St. Augustine, the most
important and significant counterconcept against this constantly threatening heresy.

[9] Romano Guardini, *The Spirit of the Liturgy,* trans. Ada Lane,
(London: Sheed & Ward, 1937), 85.

the time spent on it.[10] The *laus perennis* of the sons of St. Benedict, the festive celebration of the liturgy, which he was permitted to attend daily as an oblate of the Benedictine abbey, were for him a first schooling through which he was introduced into theology's original mysteries, the *principia* (*ST*, I, q. 1, a. 5, ad 2).

The influence of this schooling still reverberates at the close of Thomas's life. This can be seen in his prologue *Postilla super Psalmos*,[11] where he explains the singular significance of the psalms by the fact that they contain the entire contents of theology ("generalem habet totius theologiae"). These are not spread over many different books, as in the rest of the Holy Scriptures, but are concentrated in this one book; not as a narration, report, letter, or instruction, but in the most dignified form, liturgical praise, thanksgiving, and prayer. According to Thomas, wherever theology reverts to the psalms, it shows its character of wisdom in a very special way.[12]

The love of singing the psalms in the context of the divine office, founded in Monte Cassino, seems to have stayed alive within Thomas all his life. The best known of Aquinas's early biographers, William of Tocco, who

---

[10] Cf. Tommaso Leccisotti, "Il Dottore angelico a Montecassino," *RFNS* 32 (1940): 519–47; Jean-Pierre Torrell, *Saint Thomas Aquinas, Volume 1, The Person and His Work,* trans. Robert Royal (Washington, D.C.: The Catholic University of America Press, 1996).

[11] On this see Berger, *Thomas von Aquin begegnen,* 77–78.

[12] *In Psalm,* prologue. On this cf. Lydia Maidl, *Desiderii interpres. Genese und Grundstruktur der Gebetstheologie des Thomas von Aquin* (Paderborn: Schöningh, 1994), 322; and Ciro Macrelli, "La lode e il canto in San Tommaso d'Aquino," *Studi tomistici* 13 (1981): 447–53.

had the privilege of knowing Thomas personally, reports that Thomas would rise at night before the actual time for the canonical hour of Matins (cap. 34). A few chapters before (cap. 29) we read: "One also saw him often when he was singing the psalm verse during Compline in Lent: 'Do not reject us in old age, when my strength is failing,' enraptured and consumed by piety, tears streaming down his face that seemed to be bursting forth from the eyes of the pious soul."[13]

The Eucharist as the Center of Life

The undisputed center in the life of St. Thomas was the sacrament of the Eucharist, Holy Mass. William of Tocco reports (and in this he is in full agreement with all the other testimonies that are mentioned in the records of canonization): "He read one Mass a day, if he was not prevented by ill health, and heard a second one by his companion or someone else, in which he very often served at the altar. During Mass he often would be seized by such strong feelings of devotion that he dissolved in tears, because he was consumed by the holy mysteries of the great sacrament and invigorated by its offerings."[14]

---

[13] "Visus fuit etiam frequenter, cum cantaretur ille versus in Completorio quadragesimali tempore: Ne projicias nos in tempore senectutis, cum defecerit virtus mea; quasi raptus et in devotione absorptus multis perfundi lacrymis, quas de oculis videbatur educere piae mentis" (ed. Prümmer, 103–4).

[14] Cf. Martin Grabmann, *The Interior Life of St. Thomas Aquinas,* trans. Nicholas Ashenbrenner, OP (Milwaukee: Bruce, 1951). It is reported by others (such as Conradus de Suessa) that Thomas would hear two more Masses, in addition to the one he celebrated himself, in "deep prayer."

And it was also after Holy Mass, on the feast day of St. Nicholas in 1273, that the saint cast aside his writing tools and discontinued work on his theological summa, never to take it up again. "Omnia videntur mihi paleae!"

It seems likely that this silence, induced during that Holy Mass, was a mystical dumbness, which was the saint's answer to the ecstatic vision God had infused in him. Having once been blessed with this infused vision, which is but the last step to the beatific vision *(visio beata)*—so very close to that non-created, absolute, plain light of the divine existence, that light in which all divine perfections, the mildest of mercy, the most uncompromising justice and absolute freedom are wonderfully united in their one and only source—Thomas finds himself incapable of returning to the entangled, interwoven, and multifarious conclusions of the scholastic method, of returning to created theology. No longer is his eye that of the night bird, whose realm is the discursive darkness of temporality, but that of the eagle, who has risen high into the skies and who circles the sun in such fashion that he seems to stand still in all eternity and no longer wishes to divert his gaze from the inexhaustible abundance of the divine light.[15]

Particularly telling is Thomas's bearing in his hour of death, which shows us the saint's great humility toward the sacrament of the altar. When Thomas felt his death approaching he asked for the sacrament of viaticum. Before he received the Lord's body in the sacrament of the Eucharist he prayed: " 'I receive you as ransom for my

---

[15] Cf. Berger, "Thomas von Aquin—Lehrer der Spiritualität," 13–14.

soul, as viaticum for my pilgrimage; out of love to you I have studied, kept watch and toiled. It is you I preached and taught. I never said a word against you; should I ever have done so, I did it unawares, and I will not stubbornly defend my opinion, but if I have spoken ill about this sacrament or other things, I leave it entirely to the correction of the Holy Roman Church, in obedience to which I now depart from this life.' With the greatest piety and amidst tears Thomas continued saying until his end what he was accustomed to say at the elevation of the Lord's body: 'You are the king of glory, Christ, you are the everlasting son of the Father' (*Te Deum*)."[16]

As the redeemer, present in the Eucharist, holds such a central position in the life of Aquinas, it hardly comes as a surprise that when "he is presented in prayer or in levitation, it is before the image of the crucified one or in front of the altar, liturgical symbol of Christ."[17] As the most beautiful and significant testimony of his eucharistic piety, Thomas left us the texts on the liturgy of Corpus Christi and the hymn *Adoro Te*, which he wrote on

---

[16] Tocco, *Vita,* 58: "Sumo te pretium redemptionis animae meae, sumo te viaticum peregrinationis meae, pro cuius amore studui, vigilavi, et laboravi, te praedicavi et docui, nihil contra te dixi unquam, sed si quid dixi, ignorans dixi nec sum pertinax in sensu meo sed si quid male dixi de hoc Sacramento et aliis, totum relinquo correctioni Sanctae Romanae Ecclesiae, in cuius oboedientia nunc transeo ex hac vita—Dicitur etiam de praedicto Doctore, quod in elevatione Corporis Domini nostri consueverat dicere: 'Tu Rex gloriae Christe, Tu Patris sempiternus es Filius,' usque ad finem cum magna devotione et lacrimis" (ed. Prümmer, 132).

[17] Torrell, *Saint Thomas Aquinas, Volume 1, The Person and His Work,* 287.

the orders of Urban IV in Orvieto—both liturgical texts of high rank to which repeated reference will be made in what follows. One of the most renowned composers of Latin hymns of the modern age, for example, Jean-Baptiste de Santeul (†1697), said about the hymn for Lauds *Verbum supernum* that he would have gladly exchanged all his own works for these verses.[18] As Pope Pius XI put it in his circular letter *Studiorum Ducem*, on the occasion of the sixth centenary celebration of St. Thomas's canonization, "Lastly, our Doctor possessed the exceptional and highly privileged gift of being able to convert his precepts into liturgical prayers and hymns and so became the poet and panegyrist of the Divine Eucharist. For wherever the Catholic Church is to be found in the world among whatsoever nations, there she zealously uses and ever will continue to use in her sacred services the hymns composed by St. Thomas. They are the expression of the ardent supplications of a soul in prayer and at the same time a perfect statement of the doctrine of the august Sacrament transmitted by the Apostles, which is preeminently described as the Mystery of Faith. If these considerations are borne in mind . . . nobody will be surprised that St. Thomas should also have received the title of Doctor of the Eucharist."[19]

---

18 Pius Parsch, *Das Jahr des Heiles,* Vol. III (Klosterneuburg: Verlag Volksliturgisches Apostolat, 1938), 25–26.

19 Rohrbasser, *Lehre des Heils,* No. 1939.

CHAPTER 3

Liturgy as *Auctoritas* in the Theology of Thomas Aquinas

The Church's General Liturgical Practice as *locus theologicus*

THE QUESTION of the liturgy's role for theology is not only a central issue for fundamental theology *(loci theologici)*. It is also a heavily debated issue in liturgical studies ever since their birth at the turn of the seventeenth and eighteenth centuries, and even more so since the debates over the liturgical movement.[1] In his encyclical letter *Mediator Dei* (1947), Pius XII warned against interpreting the liturgy as a superordinate, independent normative principle of faith. The liturgy should rather be acknowledged as an important site for discovering the truths of faith and understanding them, a site that must take its measure from the faith of the Church.[2]

---

[1] Cf. Philippus Oppenheim, *Principia theologiae liturgicae* (Turin: Marietti, 1947), passim; P. Fernandez, "Liturgia y Teología. La historia de un problema metodológico," *Cien-Tom* 99 (1972): 135–79.

[2] AAS 39 (1947), 540–41. See Leo Scheffczyk, *Grundlagen des Dogmas. Einleitung in die Dogmatik* (Aachen: MM-Verlag, 1997), 146.

What is the position of St. Thomas on this question? For Thomas, as for the entire tradition preceding him, the liturgy's meaning and authority is certain. Like Pius XII in *Mediator Dei*, he considers liturgy as fundamentally regulated by the authority of the Church in the spirit of tradition. With this precondition—that the liturgy is an expression of the orthodoxy, which the Church protects—he is even prepared to place the liturgy, as the Church's practice, alongside Holy Scripture, and above the authority of the Fathers.[3]

By way of example, this can be seen in the question dealt with in *Secunda Secundae* (q. 10, a. 12): whether it is permissible to baptize children of Jews or other unbelievers against the will of their parents. Thomas's answer here is no, for this was never a practice of the Church *(consuetudo Ecclesiae)*. But this has "the highest authority and standing" *(maximam auctoritatem)*: "It must forever and in everything be emulated. Since the very doctrine of Catholic doctors derives its authority from the Church, we ought to abide by the authority of the Church rather than by that of an Augustine or a Jerome or of any doctor whatever."[4]

---

[3] Maidl, *Desiderii interpres,* 71–72: "Liturgy and Holy Scripture are in harmony and, taken together, are thus the highest authority for the theological argument."

[4] II–II, q. 10, a. 12: "quod maximam habet auctoritatem Ecclesiae consuetudo, quae semper est in omnibus aemulanda: quia et ipsa doctrina Catholicorum Doctorum ab Ecclesia auctoritatem habet: unde magis standum est auctoritati Ecclesiae quam auctoritati vel Augustini vel Hieronymi vel cujuscumque Doctoris. Hoc autem Ecclesiae usus numquam habuit, quod Judaeorum filii invitis parentibus baptizarentur."

Thomas employs a similar argument (albeit less happy in its outcome) when dealing with the question of the Immaculate Conception of Mary (*ST,* III, q. 27, a. 2, ad 3), where the existence of a liturgical feast day that celebrates this mystery is cited as an important criterion.[5] In the *Quaestiones de veritate* (q. 14, a. 11) the Doctor Communis had already pointed out that the only truths of faith which must explicitly be adhered to by all (educated and uneducated believers) are those "de quibus Ecclesia festa facit," which the Church's liturgy celebrates in a feast.[6]

Reference to liturgical practice can also be found, among other places, in the provisions regarding the form of administering the sacrament of Anointing of the Sick (Suppl., q. 29, a. 8) and in the question concerning the appropriate formula for consecrating the wine during Holy Mass (III, q. 78, a. 3).[7] In addition, the invocation of saints is justified by among other things the

---

[5] This is not the place to deal with the questions of Thomas's concept of the Immaculate Conception of Mary. Cf. Adolf Hoffmann, *Des Menschensohnes Sein, Mittleramt und Mutter. Kommentar zu Sth III qq.16–34* (Deutsche Thomas Ausgabe, Vol. 26), 536–49; and Garrigou-Lagrange, *La mère du Sauveur* (Paris: Cerf, 1948), 36–60.

[6] *De Veritate* q.14, a. 11: "Non tamen omnia credibilia circa Trinitatem vel Redemptorem minores explicite credere tenentur, sed soli maiores. Minores autem tenentur explicite credere generales articulos, ut Deum esse trinum et unum, Filium Dei esse incarnatum et mortuum, et resurrexisse; et alia huiusmodi, de quibus Ecclesia festa facit."

[7] *"[Q]uod Ecclesia ab apostolis instructa utitur hac forma in consecratione vini."* Cf. III, q. 60, a. 8; q. 6, 6, a. 10; q. 72, a. 4, sed contra; q. 73, a. 2, ad 1; q. 75, a. 2; q. 80, a. 12, sed contra; q. 83, a. 4.

general practice of the Church. "An additional argument is provided by the common practice of the Church which asks for the prayers of the saints in the Litany."[8]

Thus, the rite adhered to and maintained by the Church *(Ritus ab Ecclesia [con-]servatus)* is for Thomas an indisputable *auctoritas*. If objections seem to suggest a conflict between theological principle and liturgical practice, it is the theoretical principle that has to be measured by the liturgical practice, which in turn has to be measured by the teaching office of the Church.[9]

The Role of the Liturgy in the Solution of Individual Theological Questions

Given the important role which the liturgy is accorded here as *consuetudo Ecclesiae* in regard to theology, it is not surprising that in his *Summa theologiae* alone Thomas makes fifty-seven references to sections in the liturgy as evidence for what he taught. A few particularly significant and central examples are given below.

In the discussion of the question of predestination, which is important for Thomism, the issue of the number of the predestined is also raised (I, q. 23, a. 7). Setting himself apart from the many other theologians who have engaged in busy speculation over this question, Thomas finds the best solution in the liturgy: "It is, however, better to say that, 'to God alone is known the number of those

---

[8] Suppl. q. 72, a. 2: "Ad hoc est communis consuetudo Ecclesiae, quae in Litaniis sanctorum orationem petit."

[9] Walsh, "Liturgy," 560–61: "If objections suggest a conflict between principle and practice, it is the principle that has to be adjusted."

chosen to dwell in eternal happiness' [from the Oratio of the Mass for the living and the dead]."[10]

One of the most difficult issues in the doctrine of the Trinity is the question concerning the objective identification of God's existence with the relations within Him. The preface of the Most Holy Trinity and of the ordinary Sundays of the liturgical year, when the Church sings ". . . so we may adore distinction in persons, unity in being and equality in majesty,"[11] constitutes for St. Thomas an important support for the doctrine that in God existence in relations is no different from existence in essence.

The difficulties the ineffable sublimity of the mystery of the Trinity poses to the human mind are also highlighted by the theologian's struggle to find the precise verbal expression. Yet here, too, we can turn with Thomas to the teachings which the Church's liturgy offers. Thus, for example, on the question whether an expression with exclusive meaning can be accorded to a term that denotes one of the divine Persons, the use of language employed in the *Gloria* can instruct us. It says about the Son, albeit not in isolation, that he "alone is Most High," but adds in the same breath, "with the Holy Spirit, in the glory of God the Father."[12]

---

[10] Ia, q. 23, a. 7: "Sed melius dicitur, quod 'soli Deo cognitus est numerus electorum in superna felicitate locandus.'"

[11] Ia, q. 28, a. 2: "quod in Praefatione cantatur: 'Ut in personis proprietas et in essentia unitas et in majestate adoretur aequalitas.'" If we find here the term distinction rather than relation employed, this does not lessen the conclusiveness of the passage quoted, because the *proprietates* are the result of the relations.

[12] Ia, q. 31, a. 4: "quod non dicimus absolute quod solus Filius sit altissimus; sed quod solus sit altissimus 'cum Spiritu Sancto in gloria Dei Patris.'"

In the question dealing with the relation of angels to physical location, Thomas refers to the beautiful prayer at the compline, which says of the house on to which God's blessing is called: "Let thy holy angels who dwell herein keep us in peace."[13] Thomas makes recourse to the martyrology of the feast of the martyr St. Tiburtius (11 August), when he is demonstrating that the vision of truth alleviates pain and sorrow and brings forth joy. It is this very supernatural joy that the Dominicans' breviary tells us of, when it has Tiburtius exclaiming in jubilation as he walks barefoot over red-hot coals: "Methinks I walk on roses, in the name of Jesus Christ."[14] A similar point is addressed in the question whether martyrdom is an act of fortitude. Thomas answers in the affirmative and refers to the epistles for the Mass of the martyrs Fabian and Sebastian (20 January), where it says, "They became valiant in battle" (Heb 11:34).[15]

As evidence illustrating the dogma that body and soul constitute a unity in Jesus Christ, Thomas refers to the liturgy of Christmas when the Church sings: " 'Taking on an animate body, He deigned to be born of a virgin.' Therefore in Christ there was a union of soul and

---

13 Ia, q. 52, a. 1: "quod in Collecta dicitur: 'Angeli tui sancti habitantes in ea, nos in pace custodiant.' "

14 I–II, q. 38, a. 4: "Et quod est amplius, etiam inter corporis cruciatus hujusmodi gaudium invenitur: sicut Tiburtius martyr, cum nudatis plantis super ardentes prunas incederet, dixit: 'Videtur mihi, quod super roseos flores incedam in nomine Jesu Christi.' "

15 II–II, q. 124, a. 2: "Unde manifestum est quod martyrium est fortitudinis actus. Et propter hoc de martyribus legit Ecclesia: Fortes facti sunt in bello."

body."[16] Venerating Christ's cross in the adoration of submission, of *latria (adoratio latriae)*, is likewise justified by
reference to the liturgy, more precisely to the uplifting
vespers hymn of Passion Sunday *Vexilla Regis prodeunt*
(III, q. 25, a. 4).

The Liturgy for the Administration of the Sacraments and Sacramental Theology

The very nature of the case would seem to suggest that
reference to the liturgy should take pride of place in the
theology of the sacraments. Liturgical practice and direc-
tions will be systematically dealt with here and examined
in respect to their theological foundations to which they
stand in a relation of reciprocal causality.

If, for example, the matter or form of a specific sacrament is being dealt with, Thomas consults the rite for its
administration and offers an answer from that perspective. (This applies to Baptism: III, q. 66, a. 10; Penance:
Suppl., q. 28, a. 3; and Anointing of the Sick: Suppl., q.
32, a. 6). Thereby Aquinas does not only demonstrate a
profound knowledge of the liturgy, or, to be precise, the
Church Fathers' explanations of the liturgy (Ambrose and
Augustine are here again of great importance), but he also
takes care over and is well aware of the aspects pertaining
to canon law.[17] This highlights a theme that will be cov-
ered in more detail later. The physical aspect, that relating

---

[16] III, q. 2, a. 5: "secundum illud quod Ecclesia cantat: 'Anima-
tum corpus assumens de Virgine nasci dignatus est'. Ergo in
Christo fuit unio animae et corporis."

[17] Cyprian Vagaggini, *Theologie der Liturgie* (Einsiedeln: Benziger, 1959), 331.

to the body and the senses, and hence the ecclesiological aspect, plays an important part that is not cancelled out by a purely spiritual aspect on the other side.[18]

Theological explanation and the circumstances of the rite form an ingenious synthesis whenever Thomas inquires after the meaning and content of the most diverse liturgical elements. This applies to the mixing of wine and water during the offertory (III, q. 74, a. 6–8); the Eucharistic fast (III, q. 80, a. 8); concelebration (III, q. 82, a. 2);[19] the administration of communion (III, q. 82, a. 3); and the time and place of celebrating Mass (III, q. 83). Similarly, the explanation of the meaning of priestly vestments and episcopal insignia offered in the *Supplementum* (q. 40, a. 7) gives an impressive example of this.

Anyone who knows a little about psychology is aware that human beings do not simply throw away as "unnecessary" something whose meaning they are conscious of, something that "speaks to them." As long as the authority of external symbols is supported by the meaning inherent in them and characterizing them in people's awareness, this authority endures in its own right. The practical value of St. Thomas's explanations, as well as their high intrinsic theological value, becomes manifest in their pastoral power and can hardly be overestimated. The next chapter will look at these issues in more detail.

---

18 Which is insinuated with, to my mind, less than convincing argumentation by O. H. Pesch, *Thomas von Aquin,* 343.

19 On the issue of present day practice of concelebration, see Rudolf Michael Schmitz, "Inkarnation, Geschichte und Meßopfer," *Una Voce Korrespondenz* 26 (1996): 344.

CHAPTER 4

The Explanation of the Rite of the Mass in the *Summa theologiae* (III, q. 83)[1]

HE PERFECTED synthesis of the theological meaning and content and the explanation of the rite, mentioned above, is not only of great importance, but is also quite often—above all by liturgical scholars[2]—misunderstood. In this chapter therefore this synthesis will be applied to the central points of the explanation of the Mass, which Thomas compiled at the end of his life in the *Tertia pars* of his *Summa theologiae*.

The conclusion and crowning moment of the tract on the Eucharist that we find there is a *quaestio* pertaining specifically to the rite of this sacrament (III, q. 83). It is interesting to note that among Thomists only the first article of that question, that concerning the sacrificial character of Holy Mass, has attracted great interest, while the remaining questions, which constitute Thomas's

---

[1] For this cf. David Berger, "Imago quaedam repraesentativa passionis Christi—Die Erklärung des Meßritus in der *Summa theologiae* (III, q. 83) des hl. Thomas von Aquin," *Una Voce Korrespondenz* 32 (2002): 125–42.

[2] Cf. for example statements by Johannes Nebel, *Ecclesia Orans* 17 (2000): 284–86.

explanation of the Mass, have hardly been noted.[3] And this even though Thomas himself expressly underlines the importance of his observations, since in the Eucharist "the whole mystery of our salvation is comprised, therefore is it performed with greater solemnity than the other sacraments."[4]

The Sacrifice of the Mass as an Image Saturated with Reality

Including rather than excluding the other great events of salvation history, whose fulfillment it constitutes, Christ's sacrifice on the cross is the center and climax of that history, whence we receive salvation and are made members of his mystical body (III, q. 73, a. 3; *ScG* IV, c. 55). Christ the Paschal Lamb[5] and our share in it are also the keys with which Thomas elucidates the rite of the Holy Mass. Brief mention must be made here of the fact that the *Catechism of the Catholic Church* (No. 1067) follows Vatican II (*Sacrosanctum Concilium*, No. 5) and opens its explanation of the liturgy with a reference to the Paschal mystery.

The first article of a question in the *Summa theologiae* almost always lays the groundwork for answering all sub-

---

[3] Cf. for example the commentary by Réginald Garrigou-Lagrange, *De Eucharistia. Accedunt De Paenitentia quaestiones dogmaticae. Commentarius in Summam theologicam S. Thomae* (Turin: Marietti, 1946), 263–313.

[4] III, q. 83, a. 4: "quia in hoc sacramento totum mysterium nostrae salutis comprehenditur, ideo prae caeteris sacramentis cum majori solemnitate agitur."

[5] In fact Thomas understands the rites of the Holy Mass as symbolizing not only Christ's suffering, but also his resurrection. This follows quite clearly from III, q. 83, a. 5, ad 6 and 8.

sequent questions. Thus, III, q. 83, a. 1 is about the sacrificial character of the Eucharist, without developing at this point a complete theology of the sacrifice of the Mass, yet already viewing things wholly from a liturgical aspect. Two guiding perspectives are characteristic of the entire explanation of the Mass. These have already come clearly to the fore when Thomas answers the question of whether Christ is sacrificed in this sacrament.

From the first perspective, the celebration of the Eucharist is "a kind of image making Christ's passion, which is a true sacrifice of Him, present." Consequently one can rightly say, even though only in a secondary sense, that "Christ was sacrificed also in the images of the Old Testament,"[6] and that the altar is a representation of the cross and the priest in a certain sense constitutes an image of Christ (III, q. 83, a. 1, ad 2–3). Yet this first perspective is consistently combined with the second—that of the efficacy of Christ's sacrificial suffering and the bestowal of its fruits. The sacrifice of the Mass is essentially a true partaking in the sacrifice on the cross (III, q. 22, a. 6, ad 2). In it Christ is truly sacrificed "because we partake through this sacrament in the fruit of the Lord's suffering." Thomas finds his justification for this in the

---

[6] III, q. 83, a. 1: "Celebratio autem hujus sacramenti . . . imago quaedam est repraesentativa passionis Christi, quae est vera ejus immolatio. . . . Quantum igitur ad primum modum poterat dici Christus immolari etiam in figures veteris Testamenti. . . ." On the relationship between the sacrifices in the old covenant with the sacrifice of Christ according to the vision of Thomas, see III, q. 48, a. 3 and the excellent work by Matthew Levering, *Christ's Fulfillment of Torah and Temple: Salvation according to Thomas Aquinas* (Notre Dame: University of Notre Dame Press, 2002), 54–58.

Secreta of the 9th Sunday after Pentecost: There it says: "whenever the commemoration of this sacrifice is celebrated, the work of our redemption is enacted."[7] In the sacramental, objective, and visible (albeit figurative) representation of the bloody sacrifice on the cross *(imago repraesentativa)*, the offering is truly present and effective (III, q. 79, a. 7). Thomas's explanation of the rite of the Holy Mass is characterized by the combination of both elements: the invisible efficacy and causality on the one hand and, on the other, that of the figurative and visible representation and commemoration of the mysteries of Christ's life culminating in the sacrifice on the cross, the *actiones et passiones Christi* (III, q. 48, a. 6). The two elements are infused, as by a leitmotif, by what Thomas wrote in the context of the effects of the Eucharist: "Hoc sacramentum simul est et sacrificium et sacramentum" ("This sacrament is both a sacrifice and sacrament") (III, q. 79, a. 5).

We will later re-encounter the analogy to this definition of the relationship when the relationship between *signum* and *causa*, that is to say between *sacramentum* and *res*, is defined. It is above all in this fully balanced *Et–et, both–and*, relationship that Aquinas's originality in comparison with early scholasticism or even with his great contemporaries, rooted in tradition, reveals itself.[8] This

---

7 III, q. 83, a. 1: "Unde in quadam dominicali oratione secreta dicitur: Quoties hujus hostiae commemoratio celebratur, opus nostrae redemptionis exercetur."

8 Following Dom Vonier, Jacques de Lillers, in his great treatise on the relationship between sacrifice on the cross and sacrifice of the Mass, remarks that it was Thomas Aquinas's great merit to have developed a doctrine of the Eucharist without having to retract in one single item from the general definitions of the sacraments which he had given earlier; indeed the Doctor

becomes very clear from Thomas's deliberations on the
suitable time and place for celebration of the Eucharist
(III, q. 83, aa. 2–3). Before answering the associated questions, he explains: "In the celebration of this mystery, we
must take into consideration the representation of our
Lord's passion, and the participation in its fruits."[9] It is
therefore necessary to consider both elements in equal
measure *(secundum utrumque)* when determining the
suitable time and place.[10] Thus, in the first place it is
highly appropriate to offer the sacrifice of the Mass daily,
since our human weakness requires the fruits of the Lord's
passion daily. Second, as a rule the sacrament of the
Eucharist is celebrated in festive form in the time between
the third and the ninth hour, "since our Lord's passion
was enacted from the third to the ninth hour."[11]

Angelicus shows us the Eucharist as "sacrement par antono-
mase ou par excellence": Jacques de Lillers, "La Croix, la
messe, la Cène" and "La Clef de la doctrine eucharistique,"
Centre International d'Etudes Liturgiques (ed.), *Présence du
Christ dans la liturgie. Actes du sixième colloque d'études historiques, théologiques et canoniques sur le rite romain* (Paris:
C.I.E.L., 2001), 31–32.

9 III, q. 83, a. 2: "in celebratione hujus mysterii attenditur reprae-
sentatio dominicae passionis, et participatio fructus ejus."

10 Cf. III, q. 83, a. 2. On the question of the suitable place,
Thomas mentions, from the second perspective, "the reverence due to the sacrament, in which Christ is contained verily,
and not in figure only" (III, q. 83, a. 3).

11 III, q. 83, a. 2: "Quia vero domenica passio celebrata est a tertia hora usque ad nonam, ideo regulariter in illa parte diei
solemniter hoc sacramentum in Ecclesia celebratur." The times
provided here by Thomas apply—as he himself hints in the
adverbial addition *solemniter*—only for festive conventual
Masses in monastic and chapter churches. See the wonderful

The Words and Ceremonies of the Rite of the Mass

More impressive still is the consistent synthetic explanation of the eucharistic liturgy, with the help of the double principle for the explanation of the words and acts of the Mass which has been outlined, in two exceptionally elaborate articles (III, q. 83, aa. 4–5). The element of representation unfolds from three subelements that themselves flow forth from the element of the efficacy of grace. Words and ceremonies first point to some aspect of the representation of Christ's passion, then to the mystical body, the unity of which is defined in this sacrament,[12] and finally to the practical enactment of this sacrament, which is to be done in "devotion and reverence."[13]

We must limit ourselves here to one example from St. Thomas's explanation of the Mass. It is an example, moreover, that shows how much the sense of the meaning

---

explanation which Thomas provides on the symbolic meaning of time and the feast in the liturgy in Quodl. III, q. 13, a. 28.

[12] Cf. III, q. 83, a. 4, ad 6: *"quod in hoc sacramento . . . tanguntur ea quae pertinent ad populum:* the things that are mentioned in this sacrament belong to the entire Church," Thomas's remarks in his explanation of why some prayers are said aloud by the people and the priest. What in his time still sounds self-evident must today be underlined anew in the face of strange liturgical practices (in Germany, for example, Masses are held for the elderly, homosexuals, bikers, women, etc.): Mass can never be a private event—for example, for an association or for specific groups within the Church—it is always the public living enactment of the mystical body of Christ.

[13] III, q. 83, a. 5: "Et ideo in celebratione hujus mysterii quaedam aguntur ad repraesentandam passionem Christi, vel etiam dispositionem corporis mystici; et quaedam aguntur pertinentia ad devotionem et reverentiam hujus sacramenti."

of certain rites in the liturgy and the knowledge of the close connection between meaning and representative symbolism[14] had already been lost before the reform of the liturgy. Article 34 of the Constitution on the Liturgy *Sacrosanctum Concilum* says: "The rites should be distinguished by a noble simplicity; they should be short, clear, and *unencumbered by useless repetitions*."[15] When the legitimate question of what was to be understood by such "useless repetitions" was raised in the *aula* of the council hall, the reply was "repeated signs of the cross."[16] What the Council Fathers certainly had in mind were the many signs of the cross, which were made in the Roman Canon over the host and the chalice before and after the consecration. Pope Innocent III had already queried the necessity of the sign of the blessing being made over the offerings after the consecration.[17]

It is of interest to note in our context here that Thomas also took up the question of the sign of the cross. In his *Quaestio* on the rite of the sacrament of the altar he raises an objection against Innocent on his own behalf and that of Church's *consuetudo*, in accordance with the structure of

---

[14] Cf. Alfred Lorenzer, *Das Konzil der Buchhalter* (Frankfurt/Main: Fischer-Taschenbuch-Verlag, 1984), 180–93; on p. 186 Lorenzer refers explicitly to the example to be cited in the following.

[15] "Ritus nobili simplicitate fulgeant, sint brevitate perspicui et repetitiones inutiles evitent. . . ."

[16] Acta Synodalia Sacrosancti Concilii Oecumenici Vaticani II, vol. II, pars II, (Città del Vaticano, 1972), 300. Even Georg May, "Die Liturgiereform des Zweiten Vatikanischen Konzils," in Hansjakob Becker, ed., *Gottesdienst–Kirche–Gesellschaft* (St. Ottilien: Eosverlag 1991), 81, considers this example "harmless."

[17] *De sacro altaris mysterio* V, 14 (*MPL* 217, 887–88).

the scholastic *Quaestio*:[18] "The ceremonies performed in the sacraments of the Church ought not to be repeated. Consequently it is not proper for the priest to repeat the sign of the cross many times over this sacrament."[19] He answers this objection in two ways: First, he explains the consistency between and common basis of the many signs of the cross. The gestures performed by the priest in Mass are not superfluous additions, let alone ridiculous, since they are done to represent something else.[20] This also holds true of the signs of the cross: They constitute a representation of Jesus Christ's passion and sacrificial death and thus constantly point to what the Holy Mass is—a sacramental reenactment of Christ's sacrifice on the cross, with which it is substantially identical (III, q. 83, a. 1; *In Heb.* 10 *lect.* 1).[21]

Second, in his direct reaction to the objection formulated above, Aquinas answers by explaining the meaning of the sign of the cross in the tradition of explaining the Mass in terms of allegory and *rememoratio*:

> The priest, in celebrating the Mass, makes use of the sign of the cross to signify Christ's passion which

18 Cf. Pesch, *Thomas von Aquin,* 88–93.

19 III, q. 83, a. 5: "Praeterea, ea quae in sacramentis Ecclesiae aguntur, non sunt iteranda. Inconvenienter igitur sacerdos multoties iterat crucesignationes super hoc sacramentum."

20 III, q. 83, a. 5, ad 5: "ea, quae sacerdos in missa facit, non sunt ridiculosae gesticulationes; fiunt enim ad aliquid repraesentandum."

21 Cf. Bernard Lucien, "Das Opfer nach der 'Summa Theologiae' des heiligen Thomas von Aquin," Centre International d'Etudes Liturgiques, ed., *Altar und Opfer* (Paris: C.I.E.L., 1997), 34–67.

was completed upon the cross. However, Christ's passion was, so to speak, accomplished in stages. First of all, there was the handing over of Christ, which came to pass through God, through Judas and through the Jews; and this is signified by the triple sign of the cross at the words, *These gifts, these offerings, these holy unblemished oblations.* Secondly, there was the selling of Christ. Now He was sold to the priests, to the scribes, and to the Pharisees: and to signify this the threefold sign of the cross is repeated, at the words, *blessed, approved, valid*—or to signify the price for which He was sold, viz. thirty pence. In addition, a double cross is added at the words—*that it may become to us the Body and the Blood etc.,* to signify the persons of Judas the seller and of Christ who was sold. Thirdly, there was the anticipation of the Passion at the Last Supper. To denote this two further crosses are made, one in consecrating the Body, the other in consecrating the Blood; each time while *He blessed* is said. Fourthly, there was Christ's Passion itself. And so in order to represent His five wounds, there is also a fivefold sign of the cross at the words, *a pure victim, a holy victim, an unblemished victim, the holy bread of eternal life, and the cup of everlasting salvation.* Fifthly, the stretching of Christ's body on the cross, the shedding of the blood, and the fruits of the Passion, are represented by the triple sign of the cross at the words, *as many as shall receive the Body and Blood, may be filled with every blessing, etc.* Sixthly, Christ's threefold prayer upon the cross is represented; one for His persecutors when He said, *Father, forgive them;* the second for deliverance from death, when He cried, *My God, My God, why hast Thou forsaken me?* The third refers to His entrance into glory, when He said, *Father, into Thy hands I commend my spirit;* and in order to denote this there is a triple sign of the cross made at the words, *Thou dost sanctify, quicken, bless* etc. Seventhly, the three hours during which He hung upon the cross, that is, from the sixth to the ninth hour, are represented; in signification of which we make once more a triple sign of the cross at the words, *Through Him, and with Him, and in Him.* Eighthly, the separation of His soul from the body is signified by the two subsequent crosses made over the chalice. Ninthly, the resurrection on the third day is represented by the three crosses made at the words—*May the peace of the Lord be always with you.* In short, we may say that the consecration of this sacrament, and the acceptance of this sacrifice, and its fruits, proceed from the virtue of the cross of Christ, and therefore wherever mention is made of these, the priest makes use of the sign of the cross. (III, q. 83, a. 5, ad 3)

Because the substantial identity of the sacrifice on the cross and the sacrifice of the Mass are the center of the liturgy, these signs of the cross always refer to this center. Therefore, the objection, which Thomas raises in the article referred to, that when after consecration Christ is present in the form of bread and wine it is unsuitable for the priest to bless them with the sign of the cross, makes no sense. For he does not make the sign of the cross to bless or to consecrate, but "to call to mind the virtue of the cross and the manner of Christ's suffering."[22] St. Thomas provides similar impressive and at the same time memorable explanations on the priest spreading out his arms after the consecration, which is linked to Christ's outstretched arms upon the cross, on the priest's genuflecting during the canon to denote the humility and obedience with which Christ suffered, on the breaking of the host, the burning of incense, the priest's washing of hands at the offertory etc. (III, q. 83, a. 5, ad 1–12)

These ceremonies at all times recall in their concrete representation a mystery in the life of Jesus that has its center in the paschal mystery. Just as none of Jesus' acts, the *mysteria vitae Christi*, were incidental or peripheral,[23] so none of the ceremonies of the liturgy are superfluous or "unnecessary," as they all refer to a mystery in the life of Jesus and so make the strength of that life effectively present for human salvation.[24]

Each Rubric of the Missal "An Angel"

As has already been mentioned, in all these instances Thomas refers back to the explanation of the Mass based

---

[22] III, q. 83, a. 5, ad 4: "quod sacerdos post consecrationem non utitur crucesignatione ad benedicendum et consecrandum, sed solum ad commemorandum virtutem crucis, et modum passionis Christi."

[23] Cf. Richard Schenk, *"Omnis Christi actio nostra est instructio.* The Deeds and Sayings of Jesus as Revelation in the View of Aquinas," *Studi tomistici* 37 (1990): 104–31.

[24] III, q. 48, a. 6: "Omnes actiones et passiones Christi instrumentaliter operantur in virtute divinitatis ad saltuem humanam." Cf. *In I Thess.* IV, lect. 2.

on the concepts of allegory and *rememoratio*. One has to
assume that Thomas does not simply adopt this tradition
uncritically but does so deliberately. That is because this
manner of explaining the Mass has been riven by contro-
versy since its origin in the ninth century; at the time of
St. Thomas it was in one of its deepest crises due to the
dialectical opposition between symbol and reality initi-
ated by Berengar. This crisis was not, however, accidental
in its origin. It was provoked by the extravagant interpretations of certain symbolists who, in their pious fantasies,
had occasionally strayed far from their theological start-
ing point and had thereby brought about the counter-
movement of the extreme dialecticians for whom nothing
but the notion of causal efficacy was of interest.[25] This
paved the way to a one-sided, purely juridical understanding of liturgy, one which sought merely to find the
minimum requirements for the validity of the liturgical
act.[26] Yet it is characteristic of Thomas that he can be
termed neither a symbolist nor simply a dialectician.[27]
As we have seen, the Angelic Doctor succeeds here, too,
in sounding out the depths of the *media via* of Catholic

---

[25] On this cf. Albert Fries, "Einfluß des Thomas auf liturgisches
und homiletisches Schrifttum des 13. Jahrhunderts," in Willehad Paul Eckert, ed., *Thomas von Aquino. Interpretation und
Rezeption* (Mainz: Grünewald, 1974), 309–454.

[26] Cf. Henri de Lubac, *Corpus mysticum. Kirche und Eucharistie
im Mittelalter. Eine historische Studie* (Einsiedeln: Benziger,
1969), 279–301.

[27] Jungmann is of a different opinion here; he blames Aquinas
for having made too sweeping concessions to the allegorical
interpretation: *Missarum Sollemnia,* Vol. I (Vienna: Herder,
1949), 145.

thinking and putting it on display. He does so not by dissolving salvation history into an idea, but by making its condensed representation visible in liturgical place, time, and action.

What does this mean in the context of our present day situation? Renowned and influential scholars of liturgical studies, such as, for example, Joseph A. Jungmann and Adolph Franz, have come to reject Thomas's method of explaining Mass as obsolete for the twentieth century.[28] Others, however, such as the well-known Swedish historian of liturgy Alf Härdelin, advocate a rehabilitation of Thomas's approach to the liturgy. Härdelin writes: "In any case the method of interpretation alluded should be evaluated with more appreciation than has been the case hitherto. The liturgical allegoresis is an expression of the fact that in the liturgy the entire economy of salvation—with all its different dimensions of allegorical, tropological and anagogical form—is presented as a symbolic display in one single focal point."[29] The well-known German poet and winner of the Kleist Prize in 2002, Martin Mosebach, remarks on the topicality of this method: "I consider this form of interpretation exemplary. It offers the most reliable way of entirely filling a rite with prayer and of letting form and

---

[28] Joseph A. Jungmann, *Missarum Sollemnia,* I, 143–45; Adolf Franz, *Die Messe im deutschen Mittelalter. Beiträge zur Geschichte der Liturgie und des religiösen Volkslebens* (Freiburg/Breisgau: Herder, 1902), 743–40.

[29] Alf Härdelin, "Die Liturgie als Abbreviatur der Heilsökonomie," *Atti del Congresso Internazionale: Tommaso d'Aquino nel suo settimo centenario, Vol. 4: Problemi di teologia* (Naples: Ed. Domenicane, 1976), 441.

content unite into one." Mosebach goes on to offer a larger and interesting context for his statement from the history of religion: "The Hasidic Jews, those witnesses of Europe's last mystical movement, expressed the conviction that every word in their holy books is an angel. I want to learn to look at the rubrics of the missal in the same light: seeing every rule of the missal as an angel. A liturgical act, whose angel I have beheld, will never again run the danger of appearing as a soulless, formalistic, merely historical act that was dragged through times and ages to the point of utter senselessness."[30]

Whoever begins to grasp with St. Thomas what mysteries, torn from transitoriness, are articulated in the ceremonies of the liturgy in such a reality-saturated way, and how their importance is emphasized through their repetition, will also be able to fill the rite wholly with prayer and loving contemplation. He will in turn find it hardly possible to tear from the liturgy's integral structure whatever has no direct correlation with the current spirit of the age.

The Doctor Angelicus will show the way to those of whom St.-Exupéry says: "And now they yawn. On the ruins of the palace, they have laid out a public square; but once the pleasure of trampling its stones with upstart arrogance has lost its zest, they begin to wonder what they are doing here. . . . And now, lo and behold, they fall to picturing, dimly as yet, a great house with a thousand doors, with curtains that billow on your shoulders and slumberous anterooms. Perchance they

---

30 Martin Mosebach, "Was die klassische römische Liturgie für das Gebet bedeutet," *Pro Missa Tridentina* 9 (1995): 12–13.

dream even of a secret room, whose secrecy pervades the whole vast dwelling. Thus, though they know it not, they are pining for my father's palace where every footstep had a meaning. . . ."[31]

[31] Quoted from *Citadelle*, trans. Richard Howard (Chicago: University of Chicago Press, 1979), 19.

CHAPTER 5

Central Aspects of Thomist Liturgiology

THOMAS DID NOT write a "theology of the liturgy" as an independent and autonomous treatise, yet there is undoubtedly such a thing as a Thomist liturgiology. Just as philosophy is able to compile a Thomist epistemology on the basis of statements of the theme found throughout the large body of St. Thomas's work, anyone searching Aquinas for a theology of liturgy needs to refer to various sections in his great theological works—the *Commentary on the Sentences*, the *Summa contra Gentiles*,[1] and the *Summa theologiae*.[2]

Three Leitmotifs as Characteristics of Thomism

The timeless and universal meaning of Thomism lies not in particular epoch-specific and largely secondary positions,

[1] The *Summa contra Gentiles* is no "philosophical summa" but a genuine theological work: cf. Thomas S. Hibbs, *Dialectic and Narrative in Aquinas: An Interpretation of the Summa Contra Gentiles* (Notre Dame: University of Notre Dame Press, 1995). See Helmut Hoping, *Weisheit als Wissen des Ursprungs* (Freiburg/Breisgau: Herder 1997), 70–120; on the problematic issues of this work, see my review in *Lebendiges Zeugnis* 53 (1998): 314–15.

[2] Cf. Walsh, "Liturgy," 559.

although Aquinas and his school occasionally do take up such positions. That meaning is to be found in what could be described as the "leitmotifs," the guiding principles, of his philosophical and theological synthesis. These are the core theses, dominant principles, and key ideas,[3] which constitute, as it were, the Archimedean points of this school of thinking and around which a multitude of Thomas's and the Thomists' ideas and concepts of varying importance are laid as if in concentric circles: "They are the very light of Thomism and constitute his ever-present living spirit beneath the letter (Gerade sie sind das Licht des Thomismus und bilden unter dem Buchstaben seinen immerdar lebendigen Geist)."[4] We shall look briefly at three of the more general leitmotifs that are important in our context and then proceed to those leitmotifs that concern the liturgy more closely and more exclusively.[5]

Analectics as the Method of Thomism

The Freiburg philosopher Bernhard Lakebrink has pointed out that the thought not only of Hegel, typical of the modern age, but also that of Aquinas "follows a strict method, the spirit of which inspires, right down to the last detail, the constructions which are so expansively laid out and so meticulously developed."[6] Lakebrink aptly coins the term "analectics" to describe this method. "A natural

---

3 Ibid., 562. Cf. Berger, *Thomismus,* 37–45.

4 Garrigou-Lagrange, *Mystik und christliche Vollendung* (Augsburg: Literarisches Institut Haas & Grabherr, 1927), 325.

5 There is never a complete exclusiveness, as the work of St. Thomas is a complete synthesis, where every element relates to the other element in an organic metabolic exchange.

6 Bernhard Lakebrink, *Perfectio omnium perfectionum* (Città del Vaticano: Libreria Editrice Vaticana, 1984), 9.

and unconstrained bearing and equanimity toward the
cosmos, a rejection of all extremes, with a view directed
toward the whole, its priority to all its parts, whatever ten-
sions and diversity there may be within the whole—this
method of viewing everything that exists synoptically, this
antenna for the interconnections and the relationships
between all things and the organic character of existence as
a whole, this constant attempt to get down to the original
center of matters however complex and differentiated, this
mode of thinking which does not overlook anything and
which, if anything exists, fully recognizes that existence
and respects it as it should be respected . . . this we call
analectics."[7] This method is invaluable not only when in
philosophy we try to convey the concepts of act and
potency and existence and essence or when in theology we
try to find an appropriate definition of the relation
between nature and grace, reason and faith, philosophy
and theology. Likewise in Thomistic liturgiology it provides the general atmosphere—as will be seen in more
detail below—within which there can be mediation
between matter and form, body and soul, God and man,
signum and *causa*, inner content and external figure, the
latreutical and soteriological purposes of the cult, clergy,
laity, and so on.[8]

Analectics is also the foundation of Thomist aesthetics, as is seen when Thomas interprets in more detail his
original very general definition:[9] "Pulchra sunt quae visa

---

[7] Idem, *Klassische Metaphysik* (Freiburg: Rombach, 1967), 8.

[8] Walsh, "Liturgy," 579, speaks of a "balanced presence" of
these elements.

[9] On this see Grabmann, *Die Kulturphilosophie des hl. Thomas
von Aquin* (Augsburg: Benno Filser, 1925), 148–71.

placent" ("Beautiful things are those, which please when seen") (I, q. 5, a. 4, ad 1). He goes on to write: "For beauty includes three conditions, first 'integrity' or 'perfection,' since those things which are impaired are by this very fact ugly; then the due 'proportion' or 'harmony' of the parts; and lastly, 'brightness' or 'clarity,' whence things are called beautiful which have a bright color."[10] The soul of the analectical explanation of the world lies at once in the integrity, which keeps the contraries together and unites them as a whole, and also in the proportion, the structured symmetry that leads the manifold parts to a harmonious unison without abolishing their own specific character. The *claritas* is in turn itself a product of this *debita proportio*, the *splendor ordinis*: the bright shining of order (Augustine).

Beauty however is never something "from below," never designed by man for his self-glorification and dependent on his subjective feeling. (This must in any case hold true for natural beauty.) Beauty proper is the beauty of the supernatural, the beauty which is granted by the grace that cannot be merited: "Gratia divina pulchrificat sicut *lux*" ("Divine grace adorns man like the light" (*In Ps.* 23). It is not only the person who marvels in amazement at the art of Fra Angelico,[11] who reads,

---

[10] Ia, q. 39, a. 8: "nam ad pulchritudinem tria requiruntur. Primo quidem integritas sive perfectio; quae enim diminuta sunt, hoc ipso turpia sunt; et debita proportio sive consonantia; et iterum claritas. Unde quae habent colorem nitidum, pulchra esse dicuntur."

[11] Gi]ulio Carlo Argan, *Fra Angelico. Biographisch-kritische Studie* (Geneva: Skira, 1955), 9: "If however the paintings of this Dominican friar are, as we will try to show, founded on the firm

enraptured, the verses of Dante's poetry or Paul Claudel's "Le Soulier De Satin,"[12] who listens and savors the wonderful timbre of Charpentier's Vespers of the Blessed Virgin Mary or Olivier Messiaen's "Trois petites liturgies de la Présence Divine,"[13] who will encounter an attempt, largely successful, at realizing Thomist aesthetics.

The classical Roman liturgy, especially the Gregorian chant, also fulfills the criteria of Thomist aesthetic to the highest degree. Its well-structured calmness—itself the expression of an orthodox stance, assured and illuminated by grace—becomes the soul of that wonderfully shining beauty which it radiates unbroken through the changing tides of centuries and which calls out to us:

I was the yearning of all times,
I was the light of all times,
I am the fullness of all times.
I am their great assembly; I am their eternal unity.

---

basis of doctrine and hence can in a certain way be understood as the application through images of Thomistic ethics, it is hardly surprising for the brothers of St. Dominic accorded the painter the title 'Angelicus,' to designate him as the St. Thomas of painting."

12 Cf. Dominique Millet-Gérard, *Claudel thomiste?* (Paris: Champion, 1999).

13 Messiaen himself realized that no one recognized and put into words the essential meaning and directive strength of music as St. Thomas did: "Et comme dit Saint Thomas: la musique nous porte à Dieu, 'par défaut de Vérité', jusqu'au jour où Lui-même nous éblouira, par excès de Vérité. Tel est peut-être le sens signifiant—et aussi le sens directionnel—de la musique": Thomas D. Schlee et al., eds., *Olivier Messiaen. La Cité céleste* (Cologne: Wienand, 1998), 131.

I am the way of all their ways:
On me the millennia make their pilgrimage
   to God![14]

A Theocentric Sense of Mystery

All those elements which St. Thomas subsumes under
the terms *ritus ab Ecclesia servatus, consuetudo,* or *usus
Ecclesiae* and which we call the liturgy, were to the
Church Fathers simply *mysterion* or *mysteria*—mystery.[15] In order to be able to encounter the liturgy in an
appropriate manner, man needs a certain sense of mystery. St. Thomas was endowed to a high degree with
such a sense and with the ability to communicate it. It is
rightly said of him that he feared neither logic nor mystery in any great measure: "It is in fact the precision of
his logic that by necessity brings him to perceive mysteries in nature which speak of the creator in their own specific way. And it is precisely this logical perspicacity
which enables him to make other far more sublime mysteries powerfully visible: the mysteries of grace and
God's inner life, which would have remained unknown
to us without divine grace."[16]

This sense for the mystery is only possible in that
atmosphere of theocentric objectivity that is so wanting
today. The supernatural mystery is not an explication of

---

[14] Gertrud von Le Fort, *Hymnen an die Kirche* (Munich: Kösel,
   n.d.), 23.

[15] Cf. Klaus Gamber, *Fragen in die Zeit* (Regensburg: Pustet,
   1989), 42–47.

[16] Garrigou-Lagrange, *Der Sinn für das Geheimnis* (Paderborn:
   Schöningh, 1937), 9.

man's innerness, as the old and new Modernism wish to have us believe.[17] It rather approaches man from outside; man may receive it as a gift from a higher darkness. Access to the Divine is only possible for man once he has understood the antecedent status of *patiens divina*.[18] Once man has recognized this, he will come to appreciate the extent of the chasm that separates creator and creature. He will react to this recognition with the act of submissive worship so profoundly characteristic of the liturgy.[19]

Especially in the doctrine of grace that is so central to Thomas's entire theology and which we encounter in his two *Summae*, one quickly discovers, as well as an anti-Gnostic quality, an equally strong anti-Pelagian one, the best guarantee that the supernatural is maintained in its gratuitousness and not dissolved in the natural. It is not only at this point that we find modern-age anthropocentricity confronted by a consistent theocentrism.

This characteristic of Aquinas is also wonderfully articulated by Tocco (cap. 48), when he reports that St. Thomas considered it highly disconcerting when somebody preached in the homily about things other than God or that which, in their orientation toward God, may serve to uplift the soul.[20] This is something that we all

---

[17] Cf. Karl Rahner, *Foundations of Christian Faith,* trans. William V. Dych (London: Longmann & Todd, 1978), 22, "The holy mystery . . . is the one thing that is self-evident."

[18] Ia, q. 1, a. 6, ad 3: *"Hierotheus doctus est non solum discens, sed et patiens divina"* (Dionysius the Areopagite).

[19] Marie-Dominique Philippe, *Gott allein. Anbetung und Opfer* (Aschaffenburg: Pattloch, 1959), 8.

[20] "Admirabatur plurimum, ut ex eius ore frequentius est auditum, quomodo aliquis et praecipue religiosi possent de alio nisi de Deo loqui, aut de his, quae aedificationi deserviunt animarum."

too often experience in our age, totally besotted as it is with a subjectivist anthropocentricity[21] not only in the homily but also in other parts of the liturgy.

Healthy Respect for Tradition

The most painful deficiency in today's general attitude toward liturgy, besides the missing sense of what is holy and filled with mystery, is the lack of insight into the character of the liturgy as something that preserves tradition. Cardinal Stickler, having pointed out that this issue is all too often overlooked and neglected in practice, warns that the cult "ought to be preserved with greatest care, that the essential orientation must be toward preservation, with any further development being considered with great caution."[22] A precondition for this however is the healthy (i.e., analectical) respect for tradition. This is precisely what we can learn from Thomas.

Torrell's remarks about the Scholastics—originally quite general in their application, but implicitly in contrast to the theology of the present age—that they do

---

[21] Walter Hoeres, in *Gottesdienst als Gemeinschaftskult*, 9, observes most fittingly: "Firstly the direction here is also quite consistently from the theocentric to the anthropocentric. Time and again are we indoctrinated by the heralds of the permanent liturgical revolution, such as Klemens Richter in Munster, that we are to avoid the narrow confines of past ages and understand the Mass not so much as cult, as sacrifice, but much more as God's deed for man; just as if, contrary to all great theologians and all councils, we were concerned not so much with worshipping and glorifying the Almighty and accordingly with an atoning sacrifice, but above all with human well being."

[22] In Nyssen, ed., *Simandron*, 17.

not attend to their trade in isolation or strive for originality at any cost, but rather seek to be an echo of tradition, hold equally true for Aquinas.[23] The best known commentator of St. Thomas's *Summa theologiae* was well aware of this when he arrived at the conclusion— derived from his profound knowledge of Thomas's writing—that St. Thomas was able to write this grand work above all "because he was in the highest degree devoted to the ancient teachers."[24] Pope Leo XIII thought this characterization so fitting that he incorporated it into his great encyclical about Thomas, *Aeterni Patris*. While the modern age's "gallery of noble spirits" merely serves as a device for distancing oneself dialectically from them, the Doctor Angelicus admits himself into "the choir of *auctoritates* and also submits himself to them." This submission is however by no means servile and mindless: "From the distance we see him as belonging to tradition; only from close up, when we really penetrate his thoughts, can we behold the unmistakable countenance of this mind."[25]

---

[23] Torrell, *Maître spirituel,* 507: "le théologien ne pense pas en isolé et il ne recherche pas l'originalité à tout prix, il se veut l'écho d'une tradition."

[24] Thomas de Vio Cajetanus, *In II–II S.th. q. 148 a. 4 in fin* (Leon X, 1p. 74): "Thomas Aquinas . . . veteres doctores sacros quia summe veneratus est, ideo intellectum omnium quodammodo sortitus est. . . ."

[25] Wilhelm Metz, *Die Architektonik der Summa Theologiae des Thomas von Aquin. Zur Gesamtsicht des thomasischen Gedankens* (Hamburg: S. Meiner, 1998), 9.

The Unity of Man's Body and Soul and the Liturgy

Liturgy as a System of Signs

If initially one looks at the liturgy with something of a pretheological eye, it presents itself as a system of signs[26] and symbols that are accessible to the human senses. These signs do not however close themselves off in the realm of the senses. They point to those invisible spiritual realities that they seek to represent.

Faith, or more precisely the knowledge and science of faith, is required in the case of liturgy, so that this reality can be recognized as holy, that is, supernatural. Thus, the liturgy can be described in the first place as a system of signs, perceived through the senses, of a holy and invisible reality.[27]

Such a description of the liturgy comes very close to St. Thomas's teaching on the essence of the sacrament, but in this general form it applies also to sacramentals, ceremonies, and prayers:[28] "A Sacrament is defined as being the sign of a holy thing insofar as it makes men holy."[29] Over and above this characteristic of the sacrament as a

---

26 See, on the genus of the sign, Johannes a S. Thoma, *Logica* II, qq. 21–22.

27 Vagaggini, *Theologie der Liturgie,* 29–31.

28 St. Thomas also rendered great services as regards the clear distinction between the seven sacraments and the other liturgical acts of the Church. Cf. I–II, q. 108, a. 2, ad 2. Despite this distinction, however, no distinction is drawn between systematic teaching on the sacraments and liturgiology. González Fuente, "La teologia nella liturgia," 356.

29 III, q. 60, a. 2: "Et ideo proprie dicitur sacramentum quod est signum alicujus rei sacrae . . . inquantum est sanctificans homines."—cf. how this notion is taken up in the CIC No. 1084.

holy and sanctifying sign (a mediation of grace), St. Thomas and his school also regularly stress the commemorative and prognosticative element in the sacrament. Each sacrament reminds us of the atoning passion of Christ and is an anticipation of future glory (*ST*, III, q. 60, a. 3).[30] This highlights the extent to which Thomas's concept of the sacrament is consistent with his allegorical explanation of Mass. For it is the characteristic of allegory that the sphere which human beings can experience represents and displays the inaccessible sphere, that is, that the invisible is represented by what is perceived with the senses.

For Aquinas, who knew well in his thinking how to maintain and guard God's freedom, there can be no doubt that God can also lead man to eternal salvation and call him to supernatural communion with Him other than by sensually perceptible signs. Why then did he chose this way? Why is it appropriate for God to grant his holy grace in "corporal things"?[31]

Man is by Nature a Liturgical Being

It ranks among Thomas's greatest philosophical achievements—with Aristotle's help and led by divine revelation as guiding star—to have refuted those Arabic philosophers (especially Averroes) who rejected the body as an essential and integral part of the human person while at the same

---

[30] Cf. Garrigou-Lagrange, *De Eucharistia,* 153: "Sanctus Thomas ostendit quod sacramentum est signum rei sacrae sanctificantis homines, scil. gratiae quae ab eo producitur. Sed simul est commemoratio Passionis a quo derivatur et pignus seu signum prognosticum futurae beatitudinis."

[31] De art. fidei et eccl. sacr. (Marietti No. 614).

time restraining the all-too-powerful Platonic influences in
the Christian world (for example, in Origen),[32] which
could accept the body merely as punitive evil. Notwith-
standing the concrete difference between the two compo-
nents of man's substance, body and soul, the latter by
nature indestructible and immortal, for Thomas man is
nevertheless an *unum simpliciter* (I, q. 76, a. 1): a substantial unity between the soul as the actuating principle and
the body as the principle that makes concrete reality possible. The soul is the only substantial form of the body that
corresponds to primary matter. Only with the help of this
primary matter can the form unfold and perfect its dispo-
sitions (*ST*, I, a. 76, aa. 1 and 4).[33]

The Doctor Angelicus therefore emphasizes in the
most definite manner the body's, that is, matter's integral
affiliation to the human person. It is this affiliation that
naturally ennobles the body to prepare it for ascension
into the kingdom of grace. Thomas's emphasis, unusual
for his time—on the body's significance for the human
person comes naturally into its own in his consideration of
man's most noble act—the attainment of knowledge. It is
for him an irrefutable fact that all knowledge starts with
the senses *(omnis cognitio incipit a sensu)*: the unity in
essence and existence of body and soul, which we have just
discussed, reveals itself above all in human thinking.

According to scholastics influenced by Augustine,
the soul is the subject of perception through the
senses. For Thomas, however, the composite whole

32 Cf. *ScG* III, 83.
33 For this cf. DH 3616 and Robert E. Brennan, *Thomistische
Psychologie* (Heidelberg: Kerle, 1957), 64–67.

of body and soul, the entire human being, is the carrier and subject of perception through the senses.
Hence the body is involved much more with the
sense experience, which is so important and fundamental for man's entire psychic life. . . . The essence
of corporeal things is, according to Thomist epistemology, the proper object of mental knowledge, as it
is in conformity with the nature of the human subject who acquires that knowledge, which is both sensual and mental. While knowledge based on
sense-data is inherently dependent on bodily organs,
man's mental knowledge is—it is true—inherently
and subjectively independent of the body. However,
as regard the content of thinking it is still objectively
and outwardly dependent, insofar as the operation of
our intellect requires that there should be supply and
mediation through the soul's sensitive capacity, not
only for the mental knowledge of the bodily, but also
for the comprehension of purely mental objects.[34]

As Thomism holds that the same epistemological laws
apply in analogous form to the supernatural life of the
soul,[35] it is highly consistent with the nature of man that
God should communicate his grace through the visible
and beautiful signs of the liturgy so that supernatural

---

[34] Martin Grabmann, *Die Kulturphilosophie,* 47–48. Cf also DH
3619: *Cognitionem ergo accipimus a rebus sensibilibus.*

[35] Richard Marimon, *De oratione. Juxta S. Thomae doctrinam*
(Rome: Herder, 1963), 151–63. This parallelism between natural and supernatural life cycles is particularly clear in *ST,* III,
q. 65, a. 1. Even Adolf von Harnack, *Lehrbuch der Dogmengeschichte,* Vol. III (Tübingen: Wissenschaftliche Buchge-
sellschaft, 1910), 547, was enthused by this Thomist concept.

knowledge and the will as guided by grace should also have their origin there: "Now it is part of man's nature to acquire knowledge of the spiritual from the sensible. However, a sign is something by means of which someone attains to the knowledge of something else. Consequently, since the sacred things which are signified by the sacraments are the spiritual and intelligible goods by means of which man is sanctified, it follows that the sacramental signs consist of sensible things, just as in the Divine Scriptures spiritual things are set before us under the guise of things sensible. And hence it is that sensible things are required for the sacraments."[36]

From this perspective then we can say that man is by his God-given nature a liturgical being, which means that the liturgy as sensual expression of religion is connatural to man.[37] Pope Pius XII incorporated this profoundly Thomist option into his encyclical *Mediator Dei*: "The worship rendered by the Church to God must be, in its entirety, interior as well as exterior. It is exterior because the nature of man as a composite of body and

---

[36] III, q. 60, a. 2: "Est autem homini connaturale ut per sensibilia perveniat in cognitionem intelligibilium. Signum autem est per quod aliquis devenit in cognitionem alterius. Unde cum res sacrae, quae per sacramenta significantur, sint quaedam spiritualia et intelligibilia bona, quibus homo sanctificatur, consequens est ut per aliquas res sensibiles significatio sacramenti impleatur; sicut etiam per similitudinem sensibilium rerum in divina Scriptura res spirituales nobis describuntur. Et inde est quod ad sacramenta requiruntur res sensibiles. . . ."

[37] To take this to mean, as Walsh ("Liturgy," 575) does, that Thomas also endorses the cultic forms of the non-Christian religions as legitimate forms of divine worship, is to my mind an unforgiveable anachronism.

soul requires it to be so; likewise because divine Providence has disposed that 'while we recognize God visibly, we may be drawn by Him to love of things unseen.' Every impulse of the human heart, besides, expresses itself naturally through the senses."[38]

The Jubilation of the Soul, Supernaturally Endowed with Grace, that Flows over into the Body

It follows therefore from man's God-created nature that the cult, if it is to be a holistic act performed by the entire human being and if it is to enable the whole human being—as the hymn of Lauds *Verbum supernum* sings at the Corpus Christi feast—to be nurtured in his entirety,[39] constitutes an analectic unity of inner content and outward form. The 119th chapter of the third book of the *Summa contra Gentiles* is of special importance here:

> Since it is connatural to man to acquire knowledge through the senses, and since it is most difficult to arise above sensible things, divine providence has appointed sensible things as a reminder to man of things divine, so that man's intention might the more readily be recalled to divine things, not excluding the man whose mind is not equal to the contemplation of divine things in themselves. For this reason sensible sacrifices were instituted, since man offers these to God, not because God needs them, but that man might be reminded that he must refer both himself and all that is his to God

---

[38] Rohrbasser, *Heilslehre der Kirche,* No. 231.

[39] *Verbum supernum,* stanza 3: ". . . Totum cibaret hominem."

as his end, and as the Creator, Governor and Lord of all. Again, sensible things are employed for men's sanctification, in the shape of washings, anointings, meat and drink, and the uttering *(prolatione)* of sensible words, as signifying to man that he receives intelligible gifts from an external source, and from God whose name is expressed by sensible words.[40]

This perception of St. Thomas is particularly beautifully and emphatically expressed in the *Prima secundae*, where the Doctor Communis speaks of the Old Testament law and the ritual prescriptions (I–II, qq. 101–103). It is equally clear when the second part of the *Secunda* (II–II, qq. 81–100) comes to speak about religion and cult. We must restrict ourselves here again to a few examples.[41]

---

[40] *ScG* III, c.119: "Quia vero connaturale est homini ut per sensus cognitionem accipiat, et difficillimum est sensibilia transcendere, provisum est divinitus homini ut etiam in sensibilibus rebus divinorum ei commemoratio fieret, ut per hoc hominis intentio magis revocaretur ad divina, etiam illius cuius mens non est valida ad divina in seipsis contemplanda. Et propter hoc instituta sunt sensibilia sacrificia: quae homo Deo offert, non propter hoc quod Deus eis indigeat, sed ut repraesentetur homini quod et seipsum et omnia sua debet referre in ipsum sicut in finem, et sicut in Creatorem et Gubernatorem et Dominum universorum. Adhibentur etiam homini quaedam sanctificationes per quasdam res sensibiles, quibus homo lavatur aut ungitur, aut pascitur vel potatur, cum sensibilium verborum prolatione: ut homini repraesentetur per sensibilia intelligibilium donorum processum in ipso ab extrinseco fieri et a Deo, cuius nomen sensibilibus vocibus exprimitur."

[41] Cf. II–II, q. 84, a. 2 (Adoration as action of the body); ibid., a. 3 (Adoration in a definite place); ibid., q. 85 (Sacrifice as supreme act of religion).

The question whether the worship of God requires
an external act is answered by the great teacher thus:
"We pay God honor and reverence, not for His sake
(because He is of Himself full of glory to which no
creature can add anything), but for our own sake,
because by the very fact that we revere and honor
God, our mind is subjected to Him; wherein its perfection consists. Since a thing is perfected by sub-
jecting itself to its superior, for instance the body is
perfected by being quickened by the soul, and the
air by being brightened by the sun, . . . the human
mind, in order to be united to God, needs to be
guided by the sensible world . . . wherefore in the
Divine worship it is necessary to make use of corporeal things, that man's mind may be aroused thereby,
as by signs, to the spiritual acts by means of which
he is united to God."[42]

We find a similar line of argument in those passages
where the value of praying aloud is addressed. While

---

[42] II–II, q. 81, a. 7: "Respondeo dicendum, quod Deo reverentiam, et honorem exhibemus, non propter seipsum, quia ex
seipso est gloria plenus, cui nihil a creatura adjici potest; sed
propter nos, quia videlicet per hoc quod Deum reveremur, et
honoramus, mens nostra ei subjicitur: et in hoc ejus perfectio
consistit: quaelibet enim res perficitur per hoc quod subditur
suo superiori; sicut corpus per hoc quod vivificatur ab anima; et
aer per hoc quod illuminatur a sole: mens autem humana indi-
get ad hoc quod conjungatur Deo, sensibilium manuductione;
quia invisibilia Dei per ea, quae facta sunt, intellecta conspici-
untur, ut Apost. dicit Rome 1; et ideo in divino cultu necesse
est aliquibus corporalibus uti, ut eis quasi signis quibusdam
mens hominis excitetur ad spirituales actus, quibus Deo con-
jungitur." Cf. I–II, q. 101, a. 2.

praying aloud at *oratio communis* can be explained by its
ecclesial dimension, the great value of praying aloud (also
including the *oratio singularis*) is explained in more general
terms by the body–soul constitution of man. If man wants
to serve God with everything he has received from him, he
will pray not only with the mind but also with the whole
body, including the lips. Indeed the joy and jubilation of
the soul endowed with grace by God cannot do other than
let the soul's fullness flow over into the body. "Laetatum
est cor meum, et exultavit lingua mea. . . . "[43]

The question whether holy images are permitted also
fits into this context, as it is of interest from the perspective both of the history of theology and of systematics.
Thomas considers holy Scripture's use of a language rich
in images what one would expect, for man is led from the
things of the soul to those of the mind because of his
body–soul constitution. Following Dionysius, Thomas
says that God's rays cannot enlighten our limited ability
for knowledge, which forever staggers in the twilight,
"except they be hidden within the covering of many sacred
veils."[44] Another reason that Thomas enlists for the legit-
imacy of sacred images—despite Ex 20:4—is far more
profound: "But because in the New Testament God
became man, He can be adored in a corporeal image."[45]

---

43 II–II, q. 83, a. 12: "ut scilicet homo Deo serviat secundum illud
totum, quod ex Deo habet, idest non solum mente, sed etiam
corpore . . . tertio adjungitur vocalis oratio ex quadam redun-
dantia ab anima in corpus, ex vehementi affectione, secundum
illud Ps. 15: 'Laetatum est cor meum, et exultavit lingua mea.' "
See on this also Maidl, *Desiderii interpres,* 268–70.

44 I, q. 1, a. 9: "Impossibile est nobis aliter lucere divinum
radium, nisi varietate sacrorum velaminum circumvelatum."

45 III, q. 25, a. 3: "Sed quia in novo Testamento Deus factus est
homo, potest in sua imagine corporali adorari."

It is in fact only now, once man comes face to face with the incarnation of the Logos as the pivot of world history, that the paradox of the analectic unity in substance of matter and spirit, which we have described, becomes comprehensible. The incarnation of the Logos does not, however, only illuminate the connection between spirit and matter. It also directs our view toward the deepest principle of the liturgy, which we will address in the following chapters.

The God-Man and the Liturgy

Fallen Man's Return to God

Contrary to the anthropocentric shift of thinking that dominates large parts of the Catholic Church's theory and practice today, St. Thomas's entire theology is strictly theocentrically orientated.[46] As Pope John Paul II says, Thomas is justifiably honored with the title *Doctor Divinitatis*, teacher of the divine:[47] "In sacred science, all things are treated under the unifying aspect of God:

---

[46] Cf. the brilliant study by Johannes Stöhr, "Die thomistische Theozentrik der Theologie und neuzeitliche Auffassungen," *Studi tomistici* 13 (1981), 87–107. See also David Berger, *Thomismus,* 137–40. No explicit reference can be made here to the points raised in this chapter in regard to the closely related discussion over the structure and construction plan of the *Summa theologiae*: On this see Torrell, *Saint Thomas Aquinas, Volume 1, The Person and His Work,* 150–53.

[47] John Paul II, "Il metodo de la dottrina di san Tommaso in dialogo con la cultura contemporanea," Antonio Piolanti, ed., *Atti dell'VIII Congresso Tomistico Internazionale,* Vol. I (Vatican: Liberia Editrice Vaticana, 1981), 9–20.

either because they are God Himself or because they refer to God as their beginning and end."[48]

The *sacra doctrina*, the science of faith, views everything from the perspective of God, for it shares—through the revelation from whence it comes—in God's knowledge itself. (*ST*, Ia, q. 1, a. 2). God as the pure act of being, the *ipsum Esse subsistens*, subsisting Existence itself (DH 1623), is the principle and objective of all things—the Alpha and Omega of the whole creation (*Sent.* I, d. 2, div.). As in a circular movement, which is the most perfect of all movements[49]—the human being comes forth from God in creation, and this is then insolubly tied to his elevation into the state of grace; he strives and longs to return to God as the goal of all his actions and his longings.[50] This return of man to that condition from which he had once fallen in sin but to which he still inclines with a desire that is natural, ineradicable, but by itself ineffective *(desiderium naturale ex se inefficax)*,[51] is objectively made possible through

---

48 I, q. 1, a. 7: "Omnia autem tractantur in sacra doctrina sub ratione Dei: vel quia sunt ipse Deus; vel quia habent ordinem ad Deum, ut ad principium et finem."

49 *ScG* III, c.82: "motus circularis inter omnes motus est maxime perfectus."

50 II–II, q. 4, a. 2, ad 3: "finis omnium desideriorum et actionum nostrarum."

51 Cf. Thomas Aquinas, *Super Boetium De Trinitate* q. 6 a. 4 ad 5: "Quamvis enim homo naturaliter inclinetur in finem ultimum, non tamen potest naturaliter illum consequi, sed solum per gratiam, et hoc est propter eminentiam illius finis." See on this hotly debated issue Franziscus Sylvestris de Ferrara, *Comment. In S.c.G.* III, c. 51; Hermann Lais, *Die Gnadenlehre des hl. Thomas in der* Summa contra Gentiles (Munich: Karl Zink

the wonderful mystery of God's incarnation. Thomas wrote in his *Compendium of Theology*: "Lastly the Incarnation puts the finishing touch to the whole vast work envisaged by God. For man, who was the last to be created, returns by a sort of circulatory movement to his first beginnings, being united by the work of the Incarnation to the very beginning of all things."[52] In his earlier *Commentary on the Sentences*, which restructures the seemingly unsystematic construction of Peter Lombard from a strictly theocentric perspective,[53] we read: "Therefore all rivers of natural goods return to their source, when through the mystery of incarnation human nature is united with God."[54]

From the infinitely prolific root cause of all supernatural life, the life of the threefold God, grace flows forth into the redeemed through the medium of Christ's human nature. In the hypostasis of the Logos, Christ's human nature is substantially united with the divine nature in a unique way, and this is for all of us the way to the Father.[55]

Verlag, 1951), 39–67; Yves Floucat, *Vocation de l'homme et sagesse chrétienne* (Paris: Editions Saint Paul, 1989), 246–47.

[52] Comp. theol. 201: "Perficitur etiam per hoc quodam modo totius operis divini universitas, dum homo, qui est ultimus creatus, circulo quodam in suum redit principium, ipsi rerum principio per opus incarnationis unitus." trans. Cyril Vollert, SJ, *The Light of Faith: The Compendium of Theology of St. Thomas Aquinas* (Manchester, NH: Sophia Institute Press, 1993), 232; also *ST*, III, q. 1, a. 2, und *ScG* IV, 54.

[53] Cf. David Berger, *Thomas von Aquin begegnen,* 30–32.

[54] *Sent.* III prol: "Et ideo quando humana natura per incarnationis mysterium Deo coniuncta est, omnia flumina naturalium bonitatum ad suum principium reflexa redierunt."

[55] *Super Ioan.* VII, *lect.* 4 (Marietti No.1074): "Cum enim humanitas sit nobis via tendendi in Deum. . . ."

The Instrumental Causality of Jesus' Human Nature

Man is thus enabled to return to God through this mystery of incarnation. The divine Person bound himself to human nature out of a free gracious act of will and in view of mankind's sin. In this hypostatic union human nature fully subsists in the person of the Logos—the ultimate union between God and creature, which makes it possible for satisfaction and redemption from sin to occur in that very nature where sin was committed.[56]

St. Thomas describes the role the Father's eternal Word takes on through adopting human nature, with the help of the irreplaceable metaphysical doctrine of instrumental causality.[57] Divine nature makes use of the working of human nature "as of the operation of its tool. And in the same way human nature shares in the operation of the Divine Nature, as a tool shares in the operation of the principal agent."[58] Clearly influenced by the Greek Fathers, especially St. Cyril of Alexandria, Thomas and his school hold as a matter of fact that Christ's humanity has a physical or organic efficacy. The instrumental causality mentioned above must always be understood as being physical, that is, not merely moral: Christ's infinite

---

56 Cf. III, qq. 1–15.

57 Leo J. Elders, *Die Metaphysik des Thomas von Aquin,* Vol. I (Salzburg: Verlag Anton Pustet, 1985), 238: "The principal cause brings about the effect by its own power, while the instrumental cause does this through the power it receives from the principal cause."

58 III, q. 19, a. 1, resp: "divina natura utitur operatione naturae humanae sicut operatione sui instrumenti; et similiter humana natura participat operationem divinae naturae, sicut instrumentum participat operationem principalis agentis."

merit reaches us in physical efficacy from Christ's divinity via his sanctified humanity (III, q. 8, a. 1).[59] As this supernatural life flows immediately into the sacraments, the view taken on this preliminary Christological issue will come to play a central role in the question of the sacraments' efficacy, which is to be dealt with later.

Moreover, the Vatican II Constitution on the Sacred Liturgy, *Sacrosanctum Concilium,* places particular emphasis on this notion in the context of elucidating the essence of liturgy: "For His humanity, in union with the person of the Word, was the instrument of our salvation."[60] We should not let ourselves be unsettled by Karl Rahner's rather indiscriminate dislike of the doctrine of instrumental causality,[61] which can easily be explained as part of his system. Nor should we let ourselves be deceived by the slightly mechanical ring to modern ears of the terms "instrument" or "tool." As we have seen above, the body is like an instrument, a medium for the material realization of the soul, which we owe to God's love. In Christ, therefore, human nature is an animated instrument of the Godhead, which in insoluble union with the Godhead is given a share in the divine strength

---

[59] On this cf. the profound commentary by Dominicus a Marinis, *Expositio commentaria in tertiam partem Summae Doctoris Angelici Sancti Thomae* (Lyon: Philippi Borde & Laurent Arnaud, 1666), q. 8, a. 3, cap. 2.

[60] *Sacrosanctum Concilium,* 5: "Ipsius namque humanitas, in unitate personae Verbi, fuit instrumentum nostrae salutis."

[61] Karl Rahner, *Schriften zur Theologie,* Vol. I (Einsiedeln: Benziger 1957), 216–17: "The somewhat formalist and thin Thomist doctrine of Christ's instrumental causality." On Rahner's anti-Thomism cf. David Berger, "War Karl Rahner Thomist?" *Divinitas* 43 (2000): 155–99.

itself and which is thus ennobled in a manner hitherto unconceivable for human nature.[62] It is ennobled also because it may lead us from the visible to the invisible love of the Father.[63] This instrumental causality is the most appropriate way for mankind as well as for salvation history; a way by which Christ earns our salvation and communicates it to us.[64]

Thus the causal mediation of salvation happens through visible signs. Causality and sign relate analectically to one another here, like matter and form, body and soul in man, like act and potency in metaphysics. This lays the foundation not only for understanding incarnation as "original sacrament" (Carl Feckes), as the basis for all other sacraments and for the possibility of treating them as organically and harmonically interconnected.[65] It also allows the individual sacraments to reveal themselves as spatio-temporal images and expansions of the original sacrament of incarnation. They become "like instruments of the incarnate God who suf-

---

[62] Cf. III, q. 19, a. 1.

[63] Thomas (*ST,* II–II, q. 82, a. 3, ad 2) refers here to the preface of the Christmas feast: "ut dum visibiliter Deum cognoscimus, per hunc invisibilium amorem rapiamur."

[64] D. Van Meegeren, *De causalitate instrumentali Humanitatis Christi juxta D. Thomae doctrinam* (Romae-Venlo: Pontificium Institutum Angelicum, 1939), 179: "Dicitur Humanitas Christi divinitatis instrumentum quia Deus voluit incarnationem et redemptivam, unde inter Christi Humanitatem et nostram salutem causalis debet esse relatio, quae relatio juxta divum Thomam efficientem etiam importat causalitatem, quae instrumentalis est dicenda."

[65] Cf. Peter Walter, "Die deutschsprachige Dogmatik zwischen den beiden Vatikanischen Konzilien," in Wolf, ed., *Katholisch-theologische Disziplinen,* 159.

fered"[66] and can thus apply Christ's death as universal cause of human salvation to each particular effect (*ScG* IV, c. 56): Thus "in the sacrament the economy of the God-man concentrates itself as a microcosm of salvation."[67] While maintaining God's absolute supremacy over his creation, Thomas furthermore solves herewith in an exceptionally lucid and coherent manner one of the trickiest and most central questions of liturgiology: the coordination of sign and causality.[68]

Jesus Christ: At Once Priest, Sacrificial Gift, and God [69]

Fallen man could not return to God by virtue of his own natural effort. The return had to be earned and mediated by God himself. That, and why this happens in a way perceptible to the senses, has already been shown. Merit and mediation of this kind, which in metaphysical terms is characterized as instrumental causality, culminates, so far as the issue we are discussing here is concerned, in the priesthood of the God-man.

The actual office of the priest is to mediate between man and God, conveying the divine and presenting man's

---

[66] *ScG* IV, c. 56: "quia huiusmodi visibilia sunt quasi instrumenta Dei incarnati et passi."

[67] Franz von Paula Morgott, *Der Spender der heiligen Sakramente nach der Lehre des hl. Thomas von Aquin* (Freiburg/Breisgau: Herder, 1886), 25.

[68] Walsh, "Liturgy," 567–70.

[69] On this and the following paragraph see the contributions in Sergé-Thomas Bonino, ed., *Saint Thomas d'Aquin et le Sacerdoce. Actes du colloque organisé par l'Institut Saint-Thomas-d'Aquin les 5 et 6 juin à Toulouse* = *Revue Thomiste* 99 (1999), No. 1.

prayer and penance before God: "Now the priesthood is most befitting to Christ. For through Him are divine gifts bestowed on men. Moreover, He reconciled the human race to God."[70]

In view of his divine Person and nature, however, Christ is both the one who grants salvation and the one to whom atonement is offered.[71] This atonement and inner surrender finds its external expression for the senses in the sacrifice. The original image of all sacrifices and the sole source which makes all human sacrifice meritorious is Christ's sacrifice. "Therefore Christ himself, as man, was not only priest, but also a perfect sacrificial gift, being at the same time sacrifice for sin, sacrifice for a peace-offering, and a holocaust."[72]

As the sun shines but is not illuminated and the fire gives warmth without itself receiving heat, so Christ's eternally lasting priesthood is in its completion the source of all priesthood and his sacrifice which, once presented, need never be repeated, because its immeasurable power lasts unendingly,[73] is the image for all other sacri-

---

[70] III, q. 22, a. 1: "Hoc autem maxime convenit Christo. Nam per ipsum dona hominibus sunt collata. . . . Ipse etiam humanum genus Deo reconciliavit. . . . Unde Christo maxime convenit esse sacerdotem."

[71] III, q. 22, a. 3, ad 1: "licet Christus non fuerit sacerdos secundum quod Deus, sed secundum quod homo, unus tamen et idem fuit sacerdos et Deus. . . . "

[72] III, q. 22, a. 2: "Et ideo ipse Christus, inquantum homo, non solum fuit sacerdos, sed etiam hostia perfecta, simul existens hostia pro peccato, et hostia pacificorum, et holcaustum."

[73] III, q. 22, a. 5, ad 2: "licet passio et mors Christi de cetero non sit iteranda, tamen virtus illius hostiae permanet in aeternum."

fices.[74] The whole liturgy of the Church thus shares in the liturgy of the mysteries of Jesus' life, and it is effective only in their power.

Liturgy as a Real Act of the Eternal High Priest

Christ's sacrifice and priesthood have eternal value and duration: They span all places and times.[75] Even though Christ's temporal salvific deeds, the *actiones et passiones Christi* (III, q. 48, a. 6), are physically in the past and hence unrepeatable in their unique existence, they still retain their entire physical existence, and hence their efficacy, in a mysteriously wonderful way.

How this is possible is indeed a very difficult theological question. The astute Thomist and famous commentator on the *Tertia pars*, Bartholomew Medina, speaks in this context of a *mysterium reconditae theologiae:* "Explicare modum, quo praedictae operationes et passiones Christi operatae sint nostram salutem per modum efficientiae, pertinet ad mysterium reconditae theologiae."[76] Gotthold Ephraim Lessing despaired over how to bridge the "yawning gap" between Christ's past salvific deeds and today's mankind which is so in need of salvation.[77] The problematic aspects in the Benedictine Odo Casel's

---

[74] III, q. 22, a. 4: "Et ideo Christo non competit effectum sacerdotii in se suscipere, sed potius ipsum aliis communicare. Primum enim agens in quolibet genere ita est influens quod non est recipiens in genere illo; sicut sol illuminat sed non illuminatur, et ignis calefacit sed non calefecit. Christus autem est fons totius sacerdotii."

[75] III, q. 56, a. 1, ad 3: "quae virtus praesentialiter attingit omnia loca et tempora."

[76] In *ST*, III, q. 13, a. 2 (Ed. Cologne 1618, 402).

[77] Cf. David Berger, *Thomas von Aquin begegnen,* 156–57.

theology of mystery likewise stem from an inability to deal adequately with this particular mystery.[78]

Not so with Thomas: Christ himself, as the eternal high priest and head of his mystical body, continues in the rite of his Church that worship of God and atonement which culminates in his sacrifice on the cross and which turned his entire life into service to God: "Totus autem ritus christianae religionis derivatur a sacerdotio Christi." ("Now the whole rite of the Christian cult is derived from Christ's priesthood.") (*ST,* III, q. 63, a. 3). In the encyclical *Mediator Dei* this notion holds a central position: "Thenceforth the priesthood of Jesus Christ is a living and continuous reality through all the ages to the end of time, since the liturgy is nothing more nor less than the exercise of this priestly function."[79] *Sacrosanctum Concilium* (No. 7) and the new *Catechism of the Catholic Church* (No. 1069) contain a similar formulation: "Through the liturgy Christ, our redeemer and high priest, continues the work of our redemption in, with, and through his Church."

This reveals itself in particularly lucid form in the celebration of the sacraments.[80] Before our eyes unfolds the Church as founded by Christ, "in which no longer four, as formerly in the earthly paradise, but seven streams flow, according to the incarnational order that prevails in her. These seven streams flow forth from Christ's cross, to carry from there the salvation that

---

78 Cf. J. Gaillard, "La théologie des mystères," *RT* 57 (1957): 510–51.

79 Rohrbasser, *Heilslehre der Kirche,* No. 230.

80 SC 6. Cf. Gonzalez Fuente, "La teologia nella liturgia," 356–59.

springs forth from the heart of the God-man . . . to the end of the ages."[81]

In this context it is also worth mentioning that Thomas links the last *quaestio* (q. 59) of his Christology in the *Tertia* and the first question (q. 60), on the sacraments with the words: "After considering those things that concern the mystery of the incarnate Word, we must consider the sacraments of the Church which derive their efficacy from the word incarnate himself."[82] One has to note the frequency of the term *incarnatus* in the above passage. Christ, as word incarnate, as God-man, is the real *leiturgos*, the original minister of the sacraments, while the priest is authorized to act *in persona Christi*: "Christ produces the inward sacramental effect, both as God and as man, but not in the same way. For, as God, he works in the sacraments as author: but, as man, his operation conduces to the inward sacramental effects meritoriously and efficiently, but only instrumentally . . . just as Christ, as God, has power of authority over the sacraments, so, as man, he has the power of chief ministry."[83]

---

[81] Bernhard Dörholt, *Der Predigerorden und seine Theologie* (Paderborn: Schöningh, 1917), 119.

[82] III, q. 60, prol: "Post considerationem eorum quae pertinent ad mysteria Verbi incarnati, considerandum est de Ecclesiae sacramentis, quae ab ipso Verbo incarnato efficaciam habent."

[83] III, q. 64, a. 3: "quod interiorem sacramentorum effectum operatur Christus, et secundum quod est Deus, et secundum quod est homo; aliter tamen et aliter. Nam secundum quod est Deus, operatur in sacramentis per auctoritatem; secundum autem quod est homo, operatur ad interiores effectus sacramentorum meritorie et efficienter, sed instrumentaliter. . . . Et ideo sicut Christus, inquantum Deus, habet potestatem auctoritatis in sacramentis, ita inquantum homo habet potestatem ministerii principalis, sive potestatem excellentiae."

This shows itself in a particularly complete form in the sacrifice of the Holy Mass. The sacrifice of the Mass and the sacrifice of the cross are numerically identical as regards their substance *(quoad substantiam)*. They are linked by the identity of the sacrifice, of the primary sacrificing priest and of the objective; it is the same "numerically identical act of the most complete self-surrender to an atoning death which makes the sacrifice of the cross and the sacrifice of the Mass Christ's true cultic sacrifice, for this inner sacrificial act by the God-man continues in all eternity unchanged and ever present in the glorified Christ, analogously with his vision of God which is also forever present."[84] The sacrifice of the Mass and the sacrifice of the cross are distinguished merely by their external form of presentation *(quoad modum oblationis externae)*: once in blood on Golgotha, now in a mystical and bloodless form on our altars, where the blood and the body are sacramentally separated.[85]

St. Thomas's doctrine of liturgy as the true act of the eternal high priest is in the present state of unbridled subjectivity of great importance also for the liturgy. The safest and simplest way to guard against this loss of the objective or given reality of the liturgy is, as Walsh rightly

---

84 Franz Diekamp/Klaudius Jüssen, *Katholische Dogmatik nach den Grundsätzen des hl. Thomas,* Vol. III (Münster: Aschendorff, 1954), 206.

85 Garrigou-Lagrange, *Le Sacrifice de la Messe* (Var: Le Sainte-Baume, 1933), 4: "Les thomistes disent assez généralement: Missa et sacrificium Crucis sunt idem numerice sacrificium *quoad substantiam* (ratione hostiae oblatae, principalis offerentis ac finis), non vero *quoad modum* oblationis externae (quae nunc est incruenta, et olim fuit cruenta)."

says,[86] to show that the signs of the liturgy stem from causality, that is, are instituted by God, and are thus not a historical expression of human desires. Christian liturgy is conceivable only as a liturgy "from above," for as soon as it is primarily established and founded "from below" it turns into anthropocentric idolatry. Only if one takes this as a first principle can one, as a next step, correctly appreciate, in the sense of the Church's teaching, the much-invoked principle of *participatio actuosa*.[87]

The Sacraments' Physical and Instrumental Efficient Causality

From this follows an important characteristic of Thomist liturgiology: Neither pedagogical tricks nor considerations of pastoral theology but the basic law-like character of Christ's rite is the supreme standard of measurement for the rite of his mystical body. Just as the entire life and passion of Christ was directed primarily and comprehensively to the glorification of God, and as even the salvation of man is subordinated to this goal, likewise in the liturgy the soteriological purpose of the rite *(sanctificatio hominis)* is totally subordinated to its latreutical purpose

---

[86] Walsh, "Liturgy," 570: "The simplest way to guard against this forgetfulness of the objective, given reality of the liturgy is to specify that the signs being talked about are instituted by God. That tempers the freedom allowed to man's subjectivity."

[87] This principle is understood completely differently, that is, in the sense of Karl Rahner's anthropocentric emphasis, by Angelus A. Häußling, "Liturgiereform. Materialien zu einem neuen Thema der Liturgiewissenschaft," *Archiv für Liturgiewissenschaft* 31 (1989): 29. On this see Roberto De Mattei, "Erwägungen zur Liturgiereform," *Una Voce Korrespondenz* 32 (2002): 68–70.

(cultus divinus). The sanctification of man is directed ultimately to the service of the rite; it is man's incorporation
into the cultic glorification of God through Christ (III, q.
60, a. 5; III, q. 63, a. 6).

As all the graces Christ earned for us come to us objectively through his human nature, which remains forever
God's united instrument *(instrumentum conjunctum),* and
as thus Jesus' human nature is the physical and instrumental cause of the sanctification of mankind, so these
graces are bestowed on us subjectively and in a structured
way through the visible sacraments, which are likewise
physical and instrumental causes of the sacramental
grace.[88] Just as God took on visible human nature to
redeem mankind, he now employs the tangible signs of
the sacraments, in which he inseminates the natural elements with supernatural strength *(instrumenta separata)*
to convey and communicate the fruit of this redemption
to each concrete human being: Sprung forth from the
inner life of the Trinity, the inexhaustible source of all
graces, yet mediated through the sacraments, grace flows
into the redeemed; it does so through human nature,
which the eternal word adopted and sanctified. "The
principal efficient cause of grace now is God himself, in

---

[88] Cf. the wonderful remarks by Philippus a Ss. Trinitate, *Dispu-
tatio theologica de incarnatione* (Lyon: Borde & Arnaud,
1653), disp. 2, d. 2; V, 156: "nam haec executio est quaedam
continuatio illius imperii, sicut actus exterior continuatur cum
interiori: ita ut sint una actio completa et consumata; unde
non solum minister baptizat vel absolvit, sed etiam Christus
Dominus inquantum homo, quia illa est ejus actio exterior,
continuata cum actione interiori, qua vult et imperat ablu-
tionem vel absolutionem."

relation to whom Christ's humanity is as a natural instrument, whereas the sacrament is as a separate instrument. Consequently, the saving power must needs be derived through the sacraments from Christ's Godhead through his humanity."[89]

Thus both the explanation and the realization of salvation "are enacted according to the one and same basic law. As in objective salvation, so too in subjective salvation the redeeming, reconciling agent rests on an substratum accessible to the external senses"[90] and justifies in the noblest manner the existence of the liturgy as system of external signs, which effect inner grace by means of physical causality.[91] From this teaching by St. Thomas the doctrine of the physical efficacy of the sacraments developed, which in turn has come to be most vigorously defended by the Thomistic school as an essential consequence of its thinking. Even though there have always been theologians who claimed that St. Thomas himself never taught a physical efficacy of the sacraments, the astute editor of the *Clypeus theologiae thomisticae*, Jean Baptiste Gonet, O.P. (†1681),[92] is quite correct to write: "To doubt this [that Aquinas

---

[89] III, q. 62, a. 5: "Principalis autem causa efficiens gratiae ipse est Deus, ad quem comparatur humanitas Christi sicut instrumentum conjunctum; sacramentum autem sicut instrumentum separatum. Et ideo oportet quod virtus salutifera a divinitate Christi per ejus humanitatem in ipsa sacramenta derivetur."

[90] Franz von Paula Morgott, *Der Spender der heiligen Sakramente,* 20.

[91] Gonzalez Fuente, "La teologia nella liturgia," 401–7.

[92] On this see David Berger, "Jean Baptiste Gonet, OP," *Biographisch-Bibliographisches Kirchenlexikon* XVII (2000): 485–86.

advocates a physical efficacy of the sacraments—D. B.],
would mean to cover the sun with darkness, and as the
saying goes, to be blindfolded at midday."[93]

Of course all the great theologians of the Church,
including St. Thomas,[94] agree that the sacraments are
not merely pleasant uplifting customs but objective
means of grace, that is, they are *ex opere operato* effective.
The question, however, whether this *opere operato* is to be
understood merely morally or physically *(instrumentaliter)* is highly contested. While a merely moral efficacy is
maintained in various forms by Duns Scotus, the Scotists, and many other theologians with a leaning toward
modern Molinism (Vasquez, Lugo, Tournely), above all
though by so-called reform Catholicism and neo-Mod-
ernism,[95] the *Summa*[96] of St. Thomas and the works of
his best followers unambiguously advocate a physical
instrumental causality for the sacraments: "Some however say that they are the cause of grace not by their own
operation, but in so far as God causes grace in the soul
when the sacraments are administered. . . . But if we
examine the question properly, we shall see that according to the above mode the sacraments would be mere

---

93 *De Sacr. in Com.* (Paris: A. Bertier & G. de la Court, 1669),
disp. 3, art. 2, par. 4.

94 III, q. 62, a. 3–5; Garrigou-Lagrange, *De Eucharistia,* 3.

95 Cf. Otto Weiß, *Der Modernismus in Deutschland* (Regensburg:
Pustet, 1995), 581; David Berger, *Natur und Gnade* (Regensburg: S. Roderer, 1998), 180.

96 The fact that Thomas was as yet not so firm on this issue in
his earlier writings is noted already by Johannes a S. Thoma,
In *ST, III, Vol. IX,* q. 62, a. 1, d. 7, No. 317–319 (Paris: Vivès,
1886), 212–14.

signs. . . . Hence, according to this opinion the sacraments of the New Law would be mere signs of grace."[97]

This is decidedly too little for Thomas. He starts from the insight that Christ's human nature must be comprehended as the organ of his divinity and hence that the supernatural works of the God-man in salvation history must be understood as being physical.[98] Then, speaking of the instrumental causality of the sacraments which actualize Christ's work in the present time, he says very clearly: "The tool has a twofold action; one is instrumental, in respect of which it works not by its own power but by the power of the principal agent: the other is its proper action, which belongs to it in respect of its proper form. . . . In like manner the corporeal sacraments by their operation, which they exercise on the body that they touch, accomplish through the Divine institution an instrumental operation on the soul; for example, the water of baptism, in respect of its proper power, cleanses the body, and thereby, inasmuch as it is the instrument of the Divine power, cleanses the soul: since from soul and body one thing is made."[99]

---

[97] III, q. 62, a. 1: "Quidam tamen dicunt quod non sint causa gratiae aliquid operando, sed quia Deus, sacramentis adhibitis, in anima gratiam operatur. . . . Sed si quis recte consideret, iste modus non transcendit rationem signi. . . . Secundum hoc igitur sacramenta novae legis nihil plus essent quam signa gratiae."

[98] III, q. 13, a. 2: "Si loquamur de anima Christi, secundum quod est instrumentum Verbi sibi uniti, sic habuit instrumentalem virtutem ad omnes immutations miraculosas faciendas. . . ."

[99] III, q. 62, a.1: "quod instrumentum habet duas actiones: unam instrumentalem, secundum quam operatur non in virtute propria, sed in virtute principalis agentis: aliam autem habet actionem propriam, quae competit ei secundum pro

What at first sight looks like scholastic hairsplitting utterly out of touch with reality has in fact, like many other such questions, a great significance from the perspective of the Church's concrete life—in the case of our discussion here, in its actual living enactment in the liturgy. It follows naturally that those positions which ascribe only moral or psychological efficacy to the sacraments, consider them, and hence the entire liturgy, first and foremost pedagogical teaching tools and subsequently categorize them according to secular ideas. The Jesuit Erich Przywara wrote on this matter: "It is particularly in line with Thomism [which maintains the sacraments' physical causality] that Christian life is seen as the enactment of Christian order. Private and the popular piety are of secondary importance in comparison with the liturgy, while the sermon as pastoral or psychological instruction for concrete Christian life recedes into the background vis-à-vis the sermon as pure presentation of objective truth, and the examination of the needs of real practical life steps back behind the dogma's explanation in its own terms." The positions which assume a merely moral efficacy of the sacrament are quite different, as Przywara rightly notes. They will "emphasize the formation of the Christian life and hence attend to its individual and concrete needs, they will adapt Mass to what is

---

priam formam. . . . Et similiter sacramenta corporalia per propriam operationem, quam exercent circa corpus quod tangunt, efficiunt operationem instrumentalem ex virtute divina circa animam, sicut aqua baptismi abluendo corpus secundum propriam virtutem abluit animam, inquantum est instrumentum virtutis divinae; nam ex anima et corpore unum fit."

practical for the active participants . . . and will run the danger of activism (which will eventually peter out) and of religion being secularized."[100]

It is certainly not to overrate the importance of textbook theology to identify the deviation from the Thomistic doctrine of the physical efficacy of the sacraments as one of the main causes for the anthropocentric elements in the rearranging of liturgy and the whole fashion for desacralization connected with it.[101] As Cardinal Ratzinger has remarked, it was in the wake of the Age of Enlightenment and later through the liturgical movement with its pastoral overzealousness[102] that the new talk of making the liturgy fruitful in missionary and pedagogical areas came to play an important role in the anthropocentric reappraisal of the liturgy. "Liturgy is done entirely for people. It serves either the communication of contents or—once one has tired of the rationalisms and the banality that follow in their wake—the formation of community. . . . God really no longer plays a role there. Everything revolves around gaining and satisfying man and his demands. This way, though, faith is certainly not stirred. . . ."[103]

---

[100] Erich Przywara, "Thomismus und Molinismus," *Stimmen der Zeit* 58 (1933): 31.

[101] Josef Pieper, "Sakralität und Entsakralisierung," in *Über die Schwierigkeit heute zu glauben* (Munich: Kösel, 1974), 25–60.

[102] Pope Pius XII found himself forced to warn expressly against this "imprudent zeal for souls" in his great encyclical *Humani generis* of 1950. Rohrbasser, *Heilslehre,* 437.

[103] Joseph Cardinal Ratzinger, "Eucharistie und Mission," *Forum Katholische Theologie* 14 (1998): 83.

The Eucharist as Center of the
Whole Liturgical Cosmos

If the sacraments, or to be precise the liturgy, are understood as the spatio-temporal expansion of the mystery of incarnation, it becomes obvious that from an objective perspective *(in intentione)*[104] the sacrament of the Eucharist is the most important of all the sacraments, the source from which all other sacraments arise and the goal to which they are all ordered:

> The sacrament of the Eucharist is the greatest of all the sacraments: and this may be shown in three ways. First of all because it contains Christ himself substantially: whereas the other sacraments only contain a certain instrumental power, which is a share of Christ's power. Secondly, this is made clear by considering the relation of the sacraments to one another. For all the other sacraments seem to be directed to this one as to their end. It is especially manifest that the sacrament of Holy Orders is directed to the consecration of the Eucharist: and the sacrament of Baptism to the reception of the Eucharist: while a man is perfected into this direction also by Confirmation, so as not to abstain from this sacrament of the Eucharist out of over-great fear. By Penance and Anointing of the Sick man is also prepared to receive the Body of Christ worthily. In addition, Matrimony, at least in its sig-

---

[104] IV Sent, d. 8, q. 1, a. 3, sol. 3, ad 3: "quamvis hoc sacramentum sit quasi ultimum in perceptione est tamen primum in intentione."

nification, touches this sacrament; insofar as it sig-
nifies the union of Christ with the Church, of
which union the Eucharist is a figure. . . . Thirdly,
this is made clear by the outward rites of the sacraments. For nearly all the sacraments terminate in
the Eucharist: thus those who have been ordained
receive Holy Communion, as also do those who
have been baptized, if they be adults. . . . [105]

The Roman theologian Antonio Piolanti in his great
monograph on the sacrament of the altar—probably the
best work on the mystery of the Eucharist of recent
times—points out that Vatican II adopted this doctrine
of St. Thomas (SC Nos. 65, 71, 77) in a most felicitous

---

[105] III, q. 65, a. 3: "simpliciter loquendo, sacramentum Eucharistiae est potissimum inter alia sacramenta. Quod quidem trip-
liciter apparet: primo quidem ex eo quod in eo continetur;
nam in sacramento Eucharistiae continetur ipse Christus sub-
stantialiter; in aliis autem sacramentis continetur quaedam virtus instrumentalis participata a Christo. . . . Secundo hoc
apparet ex ordine sacramentorum ad invicem: nam omnia alia
sacramenta ordinari videntur ad hoc sacramentum, sicut ad
finem. Manifestum est enim quod sacramentum ordinis ordinatur ad Eucharistiae consecrationem; sacramentum vero baptismi ordinatur ad Eucharistiae receptionem, in quo etiam
perficitur aliquis per confirmationem, ut non vereatur se sub-
trahere a tali sacramento; per poenitentiam etiam, et extremam
unctionem praeparatur homo ad digne sumendum corpus
Christi; matrimonium etiam saltem sua significatione attingit
hoc sacramentum, inquantum significat conjunctionem Christi
et Ecclesiae, cujus unitas per sacramentum Eucharistiae figu-
ratur. . . . Tertio hoc apparet ex ritu sacramentorum. Nam fere
omnia sacramenta in Eucharistia consummantur . . . sicut patet
quod ordinati communicant, et etiam baptizati, si sint adulti."

way.[106] Following the Council and St. Thomas, the *Catechism of the Catholic Church* (No. 1324) teaches us: "The Eucharist is the source and summit of the Christian life. The other sacraments, and indeed all ecclesiastical ministries and works of the apostolate, are bound up with the Eucharist and are oriented toward it. For in the blessed Eucharist is contained the whole spiritual good of the Church, namely Christ himself, our Pasch."

The God-man himself is substantially hidden under the visible kinds of bread and wine (see *excursus*) as center and "original source"[107] of the sacramental world of the rite, the entire liturgical cosmos. St. Thomas responds to this unspeakable mystery, to this "greatest of Christ's miracles,"[108] to this supernatural *perfectio omnium perfectionum*,[109] with the wonderful hymns of the Corpus Christi liturgy. In a very special way these are the liturgical expression of the joy and jubilation that fill anyone who contemplates in all humility the original mystery of the liturgy, the most holy Eucharist: "Sacris solemniis juncta sint gaudia/ Et ex praecordiis sonent praeconia": ("Greet

---

106 Antonio Piolanti, *Il Mistero Eucaristico,* 623: "Il Concilio Vaticano, ispirandosi a S. Tommaso, presenta, in una elevata sintesi, la dottrina della centralità dell'Eucaristia e della convergenza dei sacramenti. . . ."

107 VI Homily of St. Thomas Aquinas on the Corpus Christi feast in the Roman breviary (Opusc. 57, lect.VI): "per quod spiritualis dulcedo in suo fonte gustatur. . . ."

108 Ibid.: *miraculorum ab ipso factorum maximum.*

109 IV *Sent.* d. 8, q. 1, a. 1, sol. 1, ad 1: "Fons christianae vitae est Christus et ideo Eucharistia perficit Christo coniungens, et ideo hoc sacramentum est perfectio omnium perfectionum, unde et omnes qui sacramenta alia accipiunt, hoc Sacramento in fine confirmantur."

we this mystery yearly returning—still does its history set our hearts burning") (*Sacris solemnis,* stanza 1). "Quantum potes, tantum aude:/ Quia major omni laude,/ Nec laudare suffices" ("Dare all thou canst, thou hast no song worthy his praise to prolong, so far surpassing powers like thine") (*Lauda Sion,* stanza 2). "Sit laus plena, sit sonora/ Sit jucunda, sit decora/ Mentis jubilation") ("Then be anthem clear and strong, thy fullest note, thy sweetest song, the very music of the breast") (stanza 5).

The Sacramental Character as the Christian's Participation in Christ's Priesthood

If the Christian rite is the continuation of Christ's priesthood, the question obviously arises as to how this can be possible, since Mass is performed ultimately by human beings. St. Thomas takes recourse in this question to the very old doctrine of the indelible character *(character indelebilis)*, with which the receiver of the sacraments of baptism, confirmation, and ordination is imprinted.[110] The sacraments do not serve only to sanctify; they also qualify their receiver for the Christian rite: "The sacraments of the New Law (are ordained) . . . for the perfecting of the soul in things pertaining to the Divine worship according to the rite of the Christian life. Now whenever anyone is deputed to some definite purpose he is wont to receive some outward sign thereof. . . . Since, therefore, by the sacraments men are deputed to a spiritual service

---

[110] Cf. Berger, "Die geschichtliche Entwicklung der Lehre vom character indelebilis," *Una Voce Korrespondenz* 26 (1996): 182–89.

pertaining to the worship of God, it follows that by their means the faithful receive a certain spiritual character."[111]

The Christian rite Christ started on earth—which he continues as head of the Church and which is, as it were, his mystical body—is characterized by the reception and subsequent handing on of the divine. It is to these acts of receiving (for which a *potentia passiva* is required) and handing on of the divine *(potentia activa)* that the sacramental character is orientated. "Consequently, it is clear that the sacramental character is specially the character of Christ, to whose character the faithful are likened by reason of the sacramental characters, which are nothing else than certain participations of Christ's priesthood, flowing from Christ himself."[112]

As Christ's priesthood is eternal and hence sanctification continues, as long as the object to which Christ wanted to tie this sanctification remains, likewise is the soul immortal, in its spiritual part, as the carrier of the sacramental character; consequently the sacramental char-

---

[111] III, q. 63, a.1: "sacramenta novae legis ad duo ordinantur: . . . et ad perficiendum animam in his quae pertinent ad cultum Dei secundum ritum christianae vitae. Quicumque autem ad aliquid certum deputatur, consuevit ad illud consignari. . . . Et ideo, cum homines per sacramenta deputentur ad aliquid spirituale pertinens ad cultum Dei, consequens est quod per ea fideles aliquo spirituali charactere insigniantur . . . sed ad actus convenientes praesenti Ecclesiae deputantur quodam spirituali signaculo eis insignito, quod character nuncupatur."

[112] III, q. 63, a. 3: "Et ideo manifestum est quod character sacramentalis specialiter est character Christi, cujus sacerdotio configurantur fideles secundum sacramentales characteres, qui nihil aliud sunt quam quaedam participationes sacerdotii Christi ab ipso Christo derivatae."

acter is indelibly imprinted on the soul *(character indelebiliter manet)*.

The act of receiving and handing on, *potentia activa* and *passiva*, are equally central to the solution of the question of which sacrament imprints which character. "Man is sanctified through each of the sacraments, as far as sanctity means purity from sin, which is the effect of grace. But in a special way some sacraments, which imprint a character, bestow on man a certain consecration, thus deputing him to the Divine worship . . . namely, baptism, confirmation, and holy orders. . . . It is the sacrament of Holy Orders that pertains to the sacramental agents: for it is by this sacrament that men are deputed to confer sacraments on others: while the sacrament of baptism pertains to the recipients, since it confers on man the power to receive the other sacraments of the Church. . . . In a way confirmation also is directed to the same purpose."[113] Thus to give man access to the most holy representation of Christ's eternal priesthood, he is withdrawn from the profane realm and through the sacramental character forever consecrated to the divine rite.

---

[113] III, q. 63, a. 6: "per omnia sacramenta sanctificatur homo, secundum quod sanctitas importat munditiam a peccato, quae fit per gratiam; sed specialiter per quaedam sacramenta, quae characterem imprimunt, homo sanctificatur quadam consecratione, utpote deputatus ad divinum cultum. . . . Et ideo per haec tria sacramenta character imprimitur, scilicet per baptismum, confirmationem et ordinem. . . . Sed ad agentes in sacramentis pertinet sacramentum ordinis, quia per hoc sacramentum deputantur homines ad sacramenta aliis tradenda. Sed ad recipientes pertinet sacramentum baptismi, quia per ipsum homo accipit potestatem recipiendi alia Ecclesiae sacramenta. . . . Ad idem etiam ordinatur quodammodo confirmatio."

The above extract also clearly demonstrates that in no way can one say "that priests and laymen sacrifice in equal manner but non-sacramentally, nor that they sacrifice sacramentally but in different grades, because the sacrifice of the Mass is sacramental and those on whom specific sacramental characters are bestowed are equipped and enabled to perform very different actions in the Church. This is by no means always an active ability. The character of baptism is, in contrast to the grace of baptism, purely passive. Only in the case of the other sacraments is the character an active one. Yet here too it is by no means of equal kind. . . . The laity is . . . in no way equipped with the sacramental power to share in the celebration of the sacrifice of the Eucharist, neither through the character of baptism nor through confirmation."[114]

Attention must also be paid to the exact explanation of "active participation" by the faithful in the liturgy. The community as a whole *in persona hominis* should never simply be turned into the active subject and carrier of the liturgical act, nor should the principle of *participatio actuosa* become the final criterion of a "successful form of liturgy." Otherwise, the demand for active participation—by itself justified—would indeed merely forward the cause of a radical secularization of the liturgy.[115]

The clear-cut definition of relations, which St. Thomas provides, is expressed in the classical liturgy in an unambiguous and exceedingly vivid manner.

---

[114] Mannes D. Koster, *Ekklesiologie im Werden* (Paderborn: Schöningh, 1940), 75.

[115] Cf. Michael Kunzler, "La liturgia all'inizio del terzo millennio," in Rino Fisichella, ed., *Il Concilio Vaticano II Recezione e attualità alla luce del Giubileon* (Milan: Ed. San Paolo, 2000), 217–31.

Like no theologian before or after him, St. Thomas suc-
ceeded in putting the sacramental character into a grand
synthesis and perspective. The entire sacramental world of
salvation appears there essentially and primarily ordered in
subordination to the Christian rite in which Christ continues his worship of God in us. The sacraments' other
purpose and nature—the sanctification of man—appear
in this perspective as subordinate to the Christian rite and
not the other way round. The two inseparable objectives
of the liturgy, sanctification and homage *(Heiligung und
Huldigung)*, do not simply run side by side, but have an
ordered relationship to one another; the act of grace is subordinate to the rite. (Analectic!) "It is obvious how the
entire sacramental world, indeed the whole liturgy, is
thus theocentrically influenced and molded. Within the
liturgy everything, even the sanctification of man, is orientated toward the glorification of God."[116] As we have
seen, this theocentricity is reflected preeminently in the
insight that the holy sacrifice is the heart of the liturgy, as
well as in the important role which the Church's priesthood is accorded as participation, in its proper grade, in
the priesthood of Christ, the head of the Church.

---

[116] Vagaggini, *Theologie der Liturgie,* 103.

Chapter 6

Quid Hoc Sacramento Mirabilius? Real Presence and Transubstantiation

Theological Reinterpretations and St. Thomas

ONE CAN HARDLY fail to see that both on the level of theory as well as in its corresponding practical sphere there is great insecurity as regards the way in which Christ is present in the sacrament of the altar, an insecurity that often borders on a break with tradition and which has its roots above all in the factual and terminological lack of clarity that exists in relation to the formal cause of this presence. Immediately before the Council of Trent defined, in its thirteenth session in 1552, that in the sacrament of the most holy Eucharist "the body and blood, together with the soul and divinity of our Lord Jesus Christ, and therefore the whole Christ is truly, really and substantially contained" (DH 1651), it taught: "By the consecration of the bread and wine there takes place a change of the whole substance of bread into the substance of the body of Christ our Lord and of the whole substance of wine into the substance of His blood. This change the Holy Catholic Church has fittingly and properly named transubstantiation" (DH 1642).

Ever since the modernist confusions at the start of the twentieth century, as well as during the *nouvelle théologie* in the middle of that century, attempts have been made to replace this clear definition of Trent with new interpretations. In a striking approximation toward Martin Luther the concept of substance—largely totally misunderstood—was first rejected out of hand as being obsolete for today's philosophy, and then the Tridentine term "transubstantiation," which itself is undoubtedly the key term for the entire doctrine of the Eucharist, was replaced with a new and allegedly more comprehensible *terminus technicus*. Terms such as transsignification (P. Schoonenberg), transfinalization (E. H. Schillebeeckx), or transessentiation (L. Smits) have been coined.

This is not merely a matter of "only" changing the terminology, as Romano Amerio put it so fittingly: "Above all the formulas are not covers or wrappings, but rather the expression of a naked truth . . . and it is not possible to maintain the meaning of a sentence, if one expresses it in terms drawn from another system of meaning. If the formula of faith says: 'Through transubstantiation the bread becomes Christ's body,' then the formula 'Through transfinalization the bread becomes Christ's body,' destroys the truth of faith. . . . "[1] This is the heart of the problem—regardless of whether the reinterpretations were "well meant" or born out of malicious intention. These new terms have a common denominator, a concern that was pursued in the 1960s above all by Karl Rahner and Bernhard Welte: The conversion of the eucharistic elements is

---

[1] Romano Amerio, *Iota unum* (Schönenberg: Verlag der Kirchlichen Umschau, 2000), 534.

shifted into the subjective sphere and only the character of the sign, the subjective meaning it has for me, changes. Through the shared celebration of the Eucharist, the bread merely takes on a new meaning for the participants in the table fellowship.[2]

Ever since these new approaches have come to penetrate the sphere of Catholic theology, the popes have repeatedly pointed out that they are irreconcilable with the dogma of transubstantiation and the real presence, which was solemnly affirmed at Trent. Pope Pius XII did so with particular emphasis in *Humani generis* (1950)[3] and Paul VI in his teaching document *Mysterium fidei* (1965).[4] As these new interpretations are based on a destruction of the Thomist concept of substance, an assiduous parallel reading of Aquinas is required to understand the authentic Church doctrine.

Such a necessity is founded not only on the fact that the Church has adopted the wording of Thomas's doctrine almost literally in the aforementioned Tridentine

---

[2] Karl Rahner, *Das Geheimnis unseres Christus* (Munich: Ars sacra, 1959), 12–18; idem, *Schriften zur Theologie,* Vol. IV (Einsiedeln: Benziger, 1960), 380–81; Bernhard Welte and Michael Schmaus, *Aktuelle Fragen zur Eucharistie* (Munich: Max Hueber, 1960), 190–94. On the new approaches cf. Piolanti, *Il Mistero Eucaristico,* 345–53; Brunero Gherardini, "Eucaristica ed ecumenismo," in Piolanti, *Il Mistero,* 651–55; R. Masi, "La conversione eucaristica nella teologia odierna," *Divinitas* 2 (1966): 272–315; Giovanni B. Sala, "Transubstantiation oder Transsiginifikation?," *ZKT* 92 (1970): 1–34.

[3] Cf. David Berger, ed., *Die Enzyklika "Humani generis" Papst Pius XII: 1950–2000. Geschichte, Doktrin und Aktualität eines prophetischen Lehrschreibens* (Cologne: Editiones Una Voce, 2000).

[4] AAS 57 (1965): 755.

definition. As well as the characterization of St. Thomas as *Doctor Eucharisticus*, which we have already mentioned, another reason was provided by Pope Innocent VI, who wrote in the fourteenth century: "The teachings of the Doctor Angelicus are, compared with all others (not counting the canonical scriptures) of such sharp lucidity in their terminology, of such a certainty in their expression and, connected with this, so full of truth in their conclusions and judgments, that those who followed them never strayed from the path of truth. Those who were hostile to them however were always suspected of error."[5] In midst of the mists that still dominate the general theological climate, the teachings of St. Thomas can be a mighty ray of the sun. A reference back to Thomas, who cries out in his sermon for the feast of Corpus Christi: "Quid hoc Sacramento mirabilius?" ("What greater miracle can there be that this sacrament?")[6] follows inevitably from the very nature of our theme.

Transubstantiation[7]

While the latter-day approaches mentioned above are often dominated by a misguided philosophical preoccupation, the Doctor Angelicus opens his question about the conversion of bread and wine into the body and blood of

---

5 *Sermo de D. Thoma*, quoted from Laurentius a Ponte, *In Cap. 9 Sap. Hom.* 13.

6 Opusculum 57 of the Roman edition.

7 On this paragraph, cf. Garrigou-Lagrange, *De Eucharistia,* 86–128; A. Bertuletti, *La presenza di Cristo nel Sacramento dell'Eucaristia* (Rome: Pont. Univ. Lateranense, 1969), 133–85; Piolanti, *Mistero Eucaristico,* 241–50 (an excellent depiction of Thomistic doctrine of transubstantiation).

Christ in the *Summa theologiae* (III, q. 75) with the unequivocal remark that this doctrine is a mystery in the strictest of senses and hence can be apprehended "but by faith, which rests upon divine authority."[8] The Doctor Angelicus emphasizes the *"Dogma datur"* just as clearly in his eucharistic hymns.[9] Thus, he says for example in the *Lauda Sion*: "Dogma datur Christianis/ Quod in carnem transit panis/ Et vinum in sanguinem./ Quod non capis, quod non vides/ Animosa firmat fides" ("Hear what holy Church maintaineth, that the bread its substance changeth into Flesh, the wine to Blood. Doth it pass thy comprehending? Faith, the law of sight transcending, leaps to things not understood") (11–12). This, however, in no way means that theological reason, *ratio fide illustrata,* is excluded, unduly curtailed, or suppressed. This can be seen from the many reasons of congruence that Aquinas enlists in this context to argue for a high degree of appropriateness for this mystery (III, q. 75, a. 1).

While the sacrifices of the Old Covenant merely indicate Christ, the sacrifice of the New Covenant is to be more—Christ himself is present in it: "Vetustatem

---

[8] III, q. 75, a. 1: "quod verum corpus Christi et sanguinem esse in hoc sacramento, neque sensu neque intellectu deprehendi potest, sed sola fide, quae auctoritati divinae innititur." The *Catechism of the Catholic Church* (No. 1381) has incorporated this section verbatim into its teaching on the sacramental sacrifice.

[9] See on their authenticity, which is no longer questioned today, Pierre-Marie Gy, "L'Office du Corpus Christi et S. Thomas d'Aquin," *RSPT* 64 (1980): 491–507; Torrell, *Saint Thomas Aquinas, Volume 1, The Person and His Work,* 129–36. On their theology and poetics, Sisto Teran, *Santo Tomas, Poeta del Santissimo Sacramento* (Buenos Aires: Universidad del Norte, 1979), passim.

novitas/ Umbram fugat veritas/ Noctem lux eliminate"
("Brings to end the olden rite; here, for empty shadows
fled, is reality instead; here instead of darkness, light")
(*Lauda Sion* 8). The entire Corpus Christi office, which
Thomas wrote and which is a very special arrangement
of texts from the Old and the New Testaments and from
traditional sources carefully designed to the minutest
detail, is permeated and enlivened by this notion.[10]
Christ's presence is furthermore consistent with God's
love for mankind as it become visible through the incarnation: a love that was to continue in its fullness after the
earthly life of the God-man ended, and in the lasting and
real presence of Christ himself it actually does continue.

Yet these are but reasons of congruence. Theology is
provided with the fact of Christ's presence by Christ's
words (Lk 22:19) themselves, so that theology need not
search for further proof of it. The task of theology is
rather to penetrate deeper into this great mystery, to reflect
further on the precise manner of the conversion of the
eucharistic elements and to refute the disfiguring here-
sies. It is instructive that Thomas himself in the first
quaestio instantly refutes the heresy of those who claim
that "Christ's body and blood are not in this sacrament
except as in a sign, a thing to be rejected as heretical,
since it is contrary to Christ's words."[11]

---

[10] On this cf. P. Descoutieux, "Theologie und Liturgie der
Eucharistie beim hl. Thomas von Aquin," *Una Voce Korrespondenz* 8 (1978): 18–23.

[11] III, q. 75, a. 1: "Quae quidam non attendes posuerunt corpus
et sanguinem Christi non esse in hoc sacramento nisi sicut in
signo, quod est tamquam haereticum abjiciendum, utpote
verbis Christi contrarium. . . ."

Even if Thomas has Berengar's symbolism in mind here, one cannot fail to see the highly topical character his words have for our age. With profound reflections Aquinas goes on to refute (q. 75, a. 2) the doctrine of impanation advocated by some of Berengar's followers.[12] The basis of this heresy is the false notion that there is a spatial movement of Christ from heaven into the Host, a notion that was also championed by the Nominalists with far-reaching consequences.[13] According to that notion Christ would no longer be in heaven, but would have locally joined the substance of the bread. In that case there could be no complete conversion in the full sense of the term. Likewise in the third article of question 75, Thomas refutes another notion, which the Nominalists, that is, the Scotists of the fourteenth and fifteenth centuries, also taught. This was a concept that would have made equally impossible a true alteration of substance,[14] by advocating the notion of annihilation[15] of the substances of bread and wine.

---

12 Cf. Guitmund von Aversa, D*e corporis et sanguinis Christi veritate in Eucharistia,* PL 149, 1427–1512.

13 The rejection of the real distinction between substance and accidents leads the nominalists to explain Christ's presence in the Eucharist as bread and body, wine and Christ's blood, being in the same place. Luther adopted this notion—presumably from Peter d'Ailli—thereby arriving at his doctrine of consubstantiation, which the Council of Trent rejected.

14 Piolanti, *Mistero Eucaristico,* 244: "Per S. Tommaso il concetto di annichilazione esclude quello di conversione e viceversa. . . ."

15 Thomas teaches consistently that God generally does not destroy anything. I, q. 104, a. 4: "Unde simpliciter dicendum est, quod nihil omnino in nihilum redigetur."

What all these erroneous concepts overlook is the fact that the alteration the dogma teaches is utterly different from any natural changes in that it is "entirely supernatural and effected by God's power alone."[16] The changes brought about in the realm of nature always relate only to the form and never to the whole thing, whose ultimate existence remains inherent to it however it may change. God as *actus purus et infinitus*, as the absolute unlimited reality and cause of all reality, can however comprehend, grasp, and completely transform the entire nature of a being. And this is exactly what happens in the eucharistic conversion; *in instanti,* in the timeless moment, he changes the entire substance of bread and wine into Christ's body and blood: "Hence this is not a conversion of form, but of substance; nor is it of the kind of natural movements: but, with a name of its own, it can be called 'transubstantiation.' "[17]

The mediating position the Thomistic doctrine of the real distinction between substance and accidents holds here is obvious. It becomes particularly pronounced in the explanation given for the testimony of the senses, which even after consecration perceive all the characteristics of bread and wine. What the senses perceive, however, is no more than the accidents of bread and wine, which are left behind devoid of any foundations to support them, while the substance of the bread has been

---

[16] III, q. 75, a. 4: "est omnino supernaturalis, sola Dei virtute effecta."

[17] III, q. 75, a. 4: "Unde haec conversio non est formalis, sed substantialis; nec continetur inter species motus naturalis, sed proprio nomine potest dici 'transubstantiatio'."

transformed into the essence of the body and that of the wine into the essence of the blood. While the accidents, in the appearance of bread and wine, are perceived by our senses, the substance is the specific object of our intellect: This however is protected against deception by supernatural faith.[18] "There faith will be given its place, when something visible is consumed in an invisible manner and veiled under an alien form. It is faith that protects the senses against deception, as they cannot but judge by the outer appearances familiar to them."[19]

This peculiar joining of the accidents of bread and wine with the substance of the body and blood of Jesus Christ is not only consistent with the appropriate reception of this sacrament by man, but also promotes the merits of faith. "Visus, tactus, gustus in te falllitur/ Sed auditu solo tuto creditor." ("Sight, touch, and taste in thee are each deceived, the ear alone most safely is believed") (*Adoro te* 2).

In the *Commentary on the Sentences,* Thomas had already remarked that faith is especially fostered by this sacrament, which challenges it to give its approval "not

---

[18] III, q. 75, a. 5, ad 2: "quod in hoc sacramenti nulla est deceptio; sunt enim ibi secundum rei veritatem accidentia, quae sensibus dijudicantur. Intellectus autem, cujus est proprium objectum substantia . . . per fidem a deceptione praeservatur." See on this also: Gy, "L'Office du Corpus Christi et la théologie des accidents eucharistiques," *RSPT* 66 (1982): 81–86.

[19] Sermon of St. Thomas Aquinas on Corpus Christ, 5th reading of Matins: "Accidentia autem sine subjecto in eodem subsistunt, ut fides locum habeat, dum visibile invisibiliter sumitur aliena specie occultatum; et sensus a deceptione reddantur immunes, qui de accidentibus judicant sibi notis."

only beyond reason, but even contrary to sense perception."[20] This holds true not only in the context of Jesus Christ's divine nature but also of his true human nature: "In Cruce latebat sola Deitas,/ At hic latet simul et humanitas,/ Ambo tamen credens atque confitens,/ Peto, quod petivit latro poenitens." ("God only on the Cross lay hid from view; but here lies hid at once the manhood too. And I, in both professing my belief, make the same prayer as the repentant thief") (*Adoro te* 3).

The dogma of the conversion of the Eucharistic elements is—as Thomas also emphasizes—most closely and necessarily tied to that of the real presence.[21] In his explanation of transubstantiation the Doctor Angelicus has thus laid the foundations for his closer examination of Christ's manner of existence in the sacrament of the altar. Before we proceed to that step, however, two additional important questions require specific clarification.

The first is whether Thomas can really be called the "inventor" of what subsequently was proclaimed at the Council of Trent as the dogma of transubstantiation.[22] This must clearly be answered in the negative. Yet this incorrect assessment was also in all probability one of the reasons for Luther's rejection of the dogma as "human invention" and for his having fallen into the heterodox

---

[20] IV. Sent. d. 10, q. 1, a. 1: "et maxime meritum fidei in hoc quod creduntur multa in hoc sacramento quae non solum praeter rationem sunt, sed etiam contra sensum. . . ."

[21] Cf. Vincenzo Cachia, *De natura transubstantiationis iuxta S. Thomam et Scotum* (Rome: Theses Theologicae Pontificii Colegii Angelici, 1929), 10–12.

[22] Pesch, *Thomas von Aquin,* 44.

doctrine of consubstantiation.[23] From the perspective of the history of theology, Pesch's assessment is not tenable. The term *transsubstantiatio* is already an established expression with Lanfranc in the eleventh century and in the theology of the twelfth century (Stephen of Tournai, Petrus Comestor, Magister Roland et al.). The Church's teaching office sanctioned it twenty years before Aquinas's birth.[24] To speak therefore of an "invention" of Thomas— one which Pesch even describes in a strange anachronism as "a highly modernistic theory"[25]—is totally off the mark. This is by no means to deny, however, that Thomas, as none before him, knew how to explain the dogma speculatively ("Dogma datur christianis"), where- upon the Council of Trent utilized his lucid observations in a highly prominent way.

Secondly, it is necessary to address an objection that has been raised against transubstantiation with increasing fre- quency since the 1950s. This objection says that Aquinas's and the Council of Trent's concept of substance has, in the face of modern physics, become doubtful if not totally obsolete and hence that it must be replaced by other concepts. This argument depends, however, on one crucial logical flaw. The metaphysical concept of sub- stance that is the basis of the dogma, and which is in such

---

23 Cf. Burkhard Neunheuser, *Eucharistie in Mittelalter und Neuzeit. Handbuch für Dogmengeschichte,* IV/4b (Freiburg/ Breisgau: Herder, 1963), 51–55.

24 1202 Pope Innocent in a Decretal (DH 782–784) of the Fourth Lateran Council in 1215 (DH 802). See on its devel- opment, Neunheuser, *Eucharistie im Mittelalter,* 19–24.

25 Pesch, *Thomas von Aquin,* 44.

wonderful harmony with the *sens commun*,[26] is totally
independent of the research findings of modern physics.
Modern physics rejects the concept of substance insofar as
"it merely purports to examine phenomena, i.e., the meas-
urable manifestations of nature. Obviously thinking in
the natural sciences works on a different plane of reflection from the philosophy of existence. The way physics
observes things does not mean that a substance may not
be assumed to exist on the ontological level."[27] Further,
one may even assert that modern physics basically has no
true concept of substance. Horst Seidl remarks very fittingly: "An empirical concept of substance that reduces
itself to the accidents—here to the quantifiable and quali-
fiable—is in fact none at all." He goes on to draw the correct conclusion that not only are the objections against the
concept of substance unfounded, but indeed that the classical concept of substance is imperatively required for the
orthodox explanation of the dogma of transubstantiation
and real presence, "and this in the only possible, the traditional sense of clearly distinguishing between substance
and accidents."[28] Now this is precisely what we find in
perfected form with St. Thomas.

---

[26] Garrigou-Lagrange, *De Eucharistia,* 116–20; idem, *Le sens commun. La philosophie de l'être et les formules dogmatiques* (Paris: Nouvelle Librairie Nationale, 1922), 91–98; Hans Meyer, *Thomas von Aquin* (Paderborn: Schöningh, 1961), 689: "Thomas' philosophy is the philosophy of the natural, philosophical redeemed human mind. . . ."

[27] Elders, *Die Metaphysik des Thomas von Aquin,* Vol. I, 199.

[28] Horst Seidl, "Zum Substanzbegriff der katholischen Transubstantiationslehre," *Forum Katholische Theologie* 11 (1995): 5.

The Sacramental Presence of Christ
in the Eucharist[29]

The 75th question of the *Tertia pars* is followed by a question on the manner in which Christ is present in the sacrament of the altar. Here again St. Thomas stresses with great emphasis: "The way in which Christ exists in this sacrament is entirely supernatural."[30] Neither man's natural way of knowing things, not even indeed the natural power of the intellect of the angels, suffices to find from their own power what divine revelation grants us in tangible form in the Church's dogma: "It is absolutely necessary to confess according to Catholic faith that the entire Christ is in this sacrament."[31]

To arrive at a right understanding of this presence, Thomas employs, as he has done already in the *Summa contra Gentiles* (IV, cap. 64), the differentiation between *ex vi sacramenti* and *ex naturali concomitantia*, a distinction that will come fundamentally to influence all further reflections. Christ is present in two ways: "First, as it were, by the power of the sacrament; secondly, from natural concomitance. By the power of the sacrament, there

---

[29] Concerning this paragraph, see Charles-René Billuart, *Summa Sancti Thomae hodiernis academiarum moribus accomodata,* Vol. 6 (Paris: Letouzey & Ané, n.d.), 472–77; Garrigou-Lagrange, *De Eucharistia,* 129–71; A. de Sutter, "La notion de présence et ses différentes applications dans la Somme Théologique de Saint Thomas," *Ephemerides Carmeliticae* 17 (1967): 49–69.

[30] III, q. 76, a. 7: "modus essendi quo Christus est in hoc sacramento, est penitus supernaturalis. . . ."

[31] III, q. 76, a. 1: "quod omnino necesse est confiteri secundum fidem catholicam quod totus Christus sit in hoc sacramento."

is under the species of this sacrament that into which the pre-existing substance of the bread and wine is changed, which means the substance of flesh and blood. But from natural concomitance there is also in this sacrament that which is really united with that wherein the aforesaid conversion has its aim."[32]

Thus, the human soul and divine nature of Christ are present because of a true concomitance—for after all the hypostatic union was never severed and since the resurrection the real union of Jesus' body with his soul truly continues for ever: "And therefore in this sacrament the body of Christ is present by the power of the sacrament, it is true, but His soul from real concomitance."[33] Because of the condition now of the transfigured Lord, in which the blood is not separated from the body, the body as well as the blood of Christ is present *concomitanter* under the species of the bread, and under the species of the wine the body is also present (III, q. 76, a. 2).[34] This doctrine, which was declared a dogma against the Hussites at the Council of Constance (DH 1198), is the basis for the admissibility of the communion under the species of bread alone: "Caro cibus, sanguis potus:/ Manet Christus

---

[32] III, q. 76, a. 1: "uno modo quasi ex vi sacramenti, alio modo ex naturali concomitantia. Ex vi quidam sacramenti est sub speciebus hujus sacramenti id in quod directe convertitur substantuia panis et vini praeexistens. . . . Ex naturali autem concomitantia est in hoc sacramento illud quod realiter est conjunctum ei in quod praedicta conversio terminatur."

[33] III, q. 76, a. 1: "Et ideo in hoc sacramento corpus Christi est ex vi sacramenti, anima autem Christi ex reali concomitantia."

[34] Cf. IV, *Sent.,* d. 10, a. 2; 4; *ScG* IV cap. 64; *In Joan.* VI, *lect.* 6; *In I Cor.* 11, *lect.* 6.

totus/ Sub utraque specie." ("Flesh from bread, and Blood from wine; yet is Christ, in either sign, all entire confessed to be" *(Lauda Sion)*.

This distinction also plays a vital role in the question whether the entire Christ is present in each part of the species of bread and wine. For it is *ex vi sacramenti* that the substance is of Christ's body but from the real concomitance that the extensibility of the sacrament derives. Thus not only is Christ's body there in substance, but the nature of the substance is fully present in each part of its extension: "It is manifest that the entire Christ is under every part of the species of the bread. . . ."[35] In his Corpus Christi sermon, which the Roman breviary adopted as the fifth reading of Matins, Thomas says: "It is eaten by the believers, yet it is not harmed or hurt. When the sacrament is distributed, he stays unharmed and whole in his entirety under each single particle."[36] He expresses it equally impressively in *Lauda Sion*: "Fracto demum sacramento,/ Ne vacilles, sed memento,/ Tantum esse sub fragmento,/ Quantum tot tegitur." ("Nor a single doubt retain, when they break the Host in twain! What was in the whole before; suffers change in state or form, the signified remaining one and the same for evermore.")

It follows closely from this that: "The body of Christ is not in this sacrament in the specific way of spatial dimension. Christ is in this sacrament by no means as in a

---

[35] III, q. 76, a. 3: "Et ideo manifestum est quod totus Christus est sub qualibet parte specierum panis. . . ."

[36] "Manducatur itaque a fidelibus, sed minime laceratur; quinimmo, diviso sacramento, sub qualibet divisionis particula integer perseverat."

place,"[37] but in terms of place can be defined only with respect to the sacramental species: "That place in which Christ's body is, is not empty; nor is it really filled with the substance of Christ's body, which is not there locally, but it is filled with the sacramental species, which are able to fill the place. . . ."[38] From this follows that Christ is, strictly speaking, in this sacrament in a totally unmoved manner and is moved from one place to another merely mediately, indirectly *(per accidens)*. The connection between accidents and substance should not, however, be underestimated as it is of great importance in view of the permanence of the real presence: For Christ's body "remains in this sacrament not only until the morrow, but also in the future, so long as the sacramental species remain: and when they cease, Christ's body ceases to be under them, not because it depends on them, but because the relationship of Christ's body to those species is taken away."[39]

While the accidents in the appearances of bread and wine can be seen with the eye, the body and blood of Christ, the substance as such, generally remains invisible

---

[37] III, q. 76, a. 5: "Corpus Christi non est in hoc sacramento secundum proprium modum quantitatis dimensivae . . . quod corpus Christi non est in hoc sacramento sicut in loco." Cf. *ScG* IV, cap. 63–64.

[38] Ibid., ad 2: "locus ille in quo est corpus Christi non est vacuus; neque tamen proprie est repletus substantia corporis Christi, quae non est ibi localiter . . . sed est repletus speciebus sacramentorum. . . ."

[39] III, q. 76, a. 6, ad 3: "corpus Christi remanet in hoc sacramento non solum in crastino, sed etiam in futuro, quousque species sacramentales manent; quibus cessantibus, desinit esse corpus Christi sub eis, non quia ab eis dependeat, sed quia tollitur habitudo corporis Christi ad illas species. . . ."

to the eye. Only in transfiguration, when our eyes are wholly suffused with supernatural light, will we be able to look at Christ's body and recognize it. The light of the faith in which we now in worship approach him, hidden under the veil of the species of bread, is like a chiaroscuro anticipation of this wonderful vision to come. "Jesu, quem velatum nunc aspicio,/ Oro, fiat illud, quod tam sitio: /Ut te revelata cernens facie,/ Visu sim beatus tuae gloriae." ("Jesu, whom I look at shrouded here below I beseech thee send me what I thirst for, so some day to gaze on thee face to face in light and be blest for ever with thy glory's sight") (*Adoro te* 7).

Jean-Pierre Torrell emphasizes that this eschatological tension in Thomas's doctrine of the Eucharist is of great originality and is hardly to be found in any of the other theologians of the thirteenth century.[40] This eschatological proviso also holds true for the explanation of the so-called eucharistic miracles.[41] In such appearances "Christ's proper semblance is not seen, but a figure miraculously formed either in the eyes of the beholders, or in the spatial dimensions of the sacrament itself."[42] This means, in the latter case, that individual accidents emerge which had been dormant in the extended quantity of the sacrament.

---

[40] Torrell, *Saint Thomas Aquinas, Volume 1, The Person and His Work,* 135–36.

[41] Cf. Peter Browe, "Die scholastische Theorie der eucharistischen Verwandlungswunder," *Theologische Quartalschrift* 110 (1929): 305–32.

[42] III, q. 76, a. 8, ad 2: "in hujusmodi apparitionibus . . . non videtur propria species Christi, sed species miraculose formata vel in oculis intuentium, vel etiam in ipsis sacramentalibus dimensionibus. . . ."

In the first case, moreover, one should not speak of a deception, as with such miracles God wants to clarify the dogma of Christ's continued presence in the most holy sacrament of the altar.[43]

Christ's Presence in the Eucharist and Reason

In the speculative development of Thomas's doctrine of transubstantiation, that is to say, of the real presence, we encounter a particularly impressive example of the harmonious confluence of mystery and reason, of *fides* and *ratio*. This becomes particularly clear where the Doctor Angelicus deals with the mode of existence of the accidents left behind (III, q. 77; IV *Sent.* dist. 12, q. 1, a. 1; *ScG* IV, cap. 62–63; *Quodl.* 3, a. 1, 9; *In I Cor.* 11, *lect.* 5). The real distinction between substance and accident is a fact easily comprehensible to the *sens commun*. In the natural sphere however, given the accidents' lack of independent status, a real separation between the two cannot be known. What appears as an impossibility according to the laws of nature is however made possible by a special law of grace:[44] The accidents of wine and bread that visibly persist after consecration are no longer maintained by the substance of the bread and wine, as they no longer exist. At first sight one could of course think that they are now maintained by the substance of Christ's body and blood. Yet that is an impossibility also: "Because the sub-

---

43 On this, cf. Johannes a S. Thoma, *Cursus Philosophicus: Logica* q. 23, a. 2; and Garrigou-Lagrange, *De Eucharistia,* 152–55.

44 III, q. 77, a. 1, ad 1: "nihil prohibet aliquid esse ordinatum secundum communem legem naturae, cujus tamen contrarium est ordinatum secundum speciale privilegium gratiae. . . ."

stance of the human body cannot in any way be affected by such accidents; nor is it possible for Christ's body, now that it is transfigured and cannot suffer any more, to be altered so as to receive these qualities."[45]

What remains therefore is that the sacramental species, although they retain the real existence they had hitherto, continue without a subject of inhesion: "The accidents continue in this sacrament without a subject. This can be done by Divine power: for since an effect depends more upon the first cause than on the second, God Who is the first cause both of substance and accident, can by His unlimited power preserve an accident in its existence when the substance is withdrawn whereby it was preserved in existence as by its proper cause."[46] The structured order of grace rises majestically far and wide over the realm of nature, without, of course, abolishing or disfiguring the latter. The supernatural separation of substance and accident is neither logically contradictory nor inherently impossible, as the definition of the accident merely includes the claim to an actualized existence in the substance, not the claim to existence itself. This natural

---

[45] III, q. 77, a. 1: "quia substantia humani corporis nullo modo potest his accidentibus affici; neque etiam est possibile quod corpus Christi gloriosum et impassibile existens alteretur ad suscipiendas hujusmodi qualitates."

[46] III, q. 77, a. 1: "accidentia in hoc sacramento manent sine subjecto. Quod quidem virtute divina fieri potest. Cum enim effectus magis dependeat a causa prima quam a causa secunda, Deus, qui est prima causa substantiae et accidentis, per suam infinitam virtutem conservare potest in esse accidens, subtracta substantia per quam conservabatur in esse sicut per propriam causam." Cf. Opusc. 57: "Accidentia enim sine subjecto in eodem existunt. . . ."

claim remains intact even after the supernatural conversion of the essence.[47]

Additional significant conclusions follow from this. It is the quantity and the spatial extension, as the primary accident of every body, that are immediately preserved by divine omnipotence. All other accidents are contained in this, as its nearest immediate carrier (III, q. 72, a. 2). Moreover, the species remain intact in their former existence and hence retain their former efficacy (III, q. 72, a. 3). They cannot only transform other bodies, but they also become victim themselves to dissolution *(corruptio)*: If this advances to that point where the former substance of bread and wine is also dissolved, as for example in the pulverization of the species of bread, Christ's presence also ceases (III, q. 72, a. 4).

Such a conversion of the species, however, does not result in a conversion of the heavenly body of the God-man. This is demonstrated by the breaking of the sacramental species of the host in Holy Mass, which metonymically depicts "the sacrament of the Lord's passion that happened on Christ's true body." "But it cannot be said that Christ's true body is broken. First of all, because it is incorruptible and impassible: secondly, because it is entire under every part, which is contrary to the nature of a thing broken."[48]

---

47 Cf. P. Sedlmayr, "Die Lehre des hl. Thomas von den accidentia sine subjecto remanentia," *Divus Thomas* (F) 12 (1934): 315–26.

48 III, q. 77, a. 7: "Non autem potest dici quod ipsum corpus Christi verum frangatur, primo quidem quia est incorruptibile et impassibile—Secundo quia est totum sub qualibet parte, ut supra habitum est, quod quidem est contra rationem ejus quod

Mystery, Jubilation, and Adoration

The teaching of St. Thomas is located not only between Berengar's symbolism on the one hand and the identification of Christ's Eucharistic body with its *figura* on the other, but also in the midst of today's heterodox perceptions. Yet it shows such wonderful unity with the teaching of the Church; not as compromise, but as its higher center, reflecting the eternal, divine truth as a crystal-clear lake, high in the mountains, reflects the sun. Jesus Christ's timeless presence in the Eucharist takes an unequivocal, unshakeable "precedence over our awareness and understanding here."[49] Through the clear distinction between substance and accidents that correlates so magnificently with the doctrine of transubstantiation—on which the dogma of the real presence is based—justice is not only done to logic, but it also preserves, as no other concept does, the objective supernatural reality of the mystery and defends it against subjectivization, or rather the usurpation of the divine by its materialization. The treatise is permeated by this leitmotif: Although the substance of the bread is *totaliter* and in the literal sense transformed into the body of Christ *(transsubstantiatio conversiva seu proprie dicta)* and hence Christ is *totaliter* and lastingly present, the body of Christ in no form suffers any change.[50]

The Thomist reflection, rational but illuminated by faith, proceeds profoundly and boldly, yet still like no

---

frangitur . . . ita fractio hujusmodi specierum est sacramentum dominicae passionis, quae fuit in corpore Christi vero."

[49] Seidl, *Substanzbegriff,* 16.

[50] Cf. Garrigou-Lagrange, *De Eucharistia,* I.

other bows humbly before the supernatural mystery it encounters in the dogma of the Church. Just as Thomas opens the gates to his speculative treatment of the dogma by hinting at the fact that the Holy Eucharist is a mystery in the strictest sense, so his theology flows forth into acts of praise and worship that express the appropriate bearing toward the mystery. It is not only the jubilation of the hymns of Corpus Christi that expresses this. The most impressive display is in the prayer quoted above, the one with which the great and yet humble teacher concluded his life.

CHAPTER 7

Thomas—The Man of the New Millenium

L ITURGY HOLDS a central position not only in the life of St. Thomas, as source of his holiness, but also as the basis for his theological works, where it is the *locus theologicus*. That is why the close connection between Thomas's dogmatic doctrine of the sacraments and his liturgical theology strikes such a positive note.

The philosophy and theology of Aquinas, where all the elements for a construction of a fundamental liturgiology can be found, also constitute a basis of almost unsurpassable value for a "beginning from within" so urgently required today. In Aquinas we find a liturgiology which truly correlates with a liturgy and which is "the summit toward which the activity of the Church is directed and at the same time the fount from which all her power flows" (*Sacrosanctum Concilium* 10); a liturgiology that is opposed to the greatest dangers threatening the liturgy today, namely anthropocentrism, naturalism, and pelagianizing actionism. It is precisely here, though, that its great relevance, hitherto neglected, reveals itself, as the contemporaneity of the non-contemporaneous.

Without wanting to instrumentalize St. Thomas for the purpose of Church politics, our examination has at any rate clearly shown that anyone who really wishes to understand St. Thomas must also be familiar with classical Roman liturgy[1] since it was in that environment that the work of Aquinas grew and matured and came to bear such abundant fruit. It is not necessary to have read Gadamer to know that the closer the context of comprehension within which the text is received comes to that of the author, the better the recipient will understand what the author says.[2] It seems equally obvious that Cardinal Ratzinger's demand for a "rediscovery of the living center" of Catholic liturgy—the long overdue "reform of the reform"—and Cardinal Stickler's warning that holy rites must be preserved both need to be referred above all to St. Thomas.

Franziscus Sylvestris Ferrara (†1528), the faithful interpreter of Aquinas's doctrine of grace and the famous commentator on the *Summa contra Gentiles*, described the saint as *homo omnium horarum*, a man for all hours and times. No age, however, is so in need of St. Thomas as ours. The dawning new millennium must—if it is to herald the felicitous times for which Pope John Paul II is

---

[1] Many liturgical texts, which St. Thomas refers to in his writings, have vanished after the liturgy reform or have been pushed to the margins (such as the Holy Trinity preface and the prayer for compline).

[2] Cf. Anselm Günthör, "50 Jahre 'Humani generis' und der Thomismus," in Berger, ed., *Die Enzyklika "Humani generis,"* 96–97.

hoping—be a Thomist one, not exclusively in the sphere of the liturgy, yet there especially so.

"More than ever the Doctor Angelicus comes to us in giant leaps."[3]

---

[3] Gilbert Keith Chesterton, *Thomas von Aquin,* trans. Elisabeth Kaufmann (into German) (Heidelberg: Kerle, 1957), 223 (free translation of the German translator's text, itself a freely rendered paraphrase of the original closing paragraph).

Bibliography

Abbreviations

CienTom Ciencia Tomista, Salamanca, Spain
PRMCL Periodica de re morali canonica liturgica, Rome, Italy
RFNS Rivista di filosofia neoscolastica, Milan, Italy
RSPT Revue des sciences philosophiques et theologiques,
Paris, France
RT Revue Thomiste, Toulouse, France

The abbreviation "DH" follows the German *Lexikon für Theology und Kirche,* 3rd edition (1993) and S. R. Schwertner, *Theolgische Realeuzypelopädie: Abku-aungs-verzeichius,* 2nd edition, Berlin–New York 1994 in reference to Denzinger-Hünermann *Enchiridon Symbolorum et declarationum de rebus fidei et morum.*

Amerio, Romano. *Iota Unum. Eine Studie über die Veränderungen in der katholischen Kirche im XX. Jahrhundert.* Schönenberg: Verlag der Kirchlichen Umschau, 2000.
Aquinas, St. Thomas. *The Light of Faith: The Compendium of Theology of St. Thomas Aquinas.* Translated by Cyril Vollert, SJ. Manchester, NH: Sophia Institute Press, 1993, 232.

Argan, Giulio Carlo. *Fra Angelico. Biographisch-kritische Studie.* Geneva: Skira, 1955.

Beck, Magnus. *Wege der Mystik bei Thomas von Aquin.* St. Ottilien: Eosverlag, 1990.

Berger, David. "Der heilige Thomas von Aquino und die Liturgie." *Una Voce Korrespondenz* 27 (1997): 76–84.

———. "Die letzte Schrift des hl. Thomas von Aquin." *Forum Katholische Theologie* 14 (1998): 221–30.

———. "Die Rolle französischer Thomisten aus dem Dominikanerorden in der Entwicklung der deutschsprachigen Fundamentaltheologie des 20. Jahrhunderts." *Angelicum* 77 (2000): 579–616.

———. "Imago quaedam repraesentativa passionis Christi— Die Erklärung des Meßritus in der *Summa theologiae* (III q. 83) des hl. Thomas von Aquin." *Una Voce Korrespondenz* 32 (2002): 125–42.

———. *Natur und Gnade. In systematischer Theologie und Religionspädagogik von der Mitte des 19. Jahrhunderts bis zur Gegenwart.* Regensburg: S. Roderer, 1998.

———. "Revisionistische Geschichtsschreibung. Das Alberigo-Projekt zur Geschichte des 2. Vatikanischen Konzils." *Theologisches* 29 (1999): 3–13.

———. *Thomas von Aquin begegnen (Reihe: Zeugen des Glaubens).* Augsburg: Sankt Ulrich Verlag, 2002.

———. "Thomas von Aquin—Lehrer der Spiritualität." *Der Fels* 30 (1999): 12–15.

———. *Thomismus. Große Leitmotive der thomistischen Synthese und ihre Aktualität für die Gegenwart.* Cologne: Editiones Thomisticae, 2001.

———. "War Karl Rahner Thomist? Überlegungen anhand der Rahnerschen Gnadenlehre," *Divinitas* 43 (2000): 155–99.

————, Editor. *Die Enzyklika "Humani generis" Papst Pius' XII 1950–2000. Geschichte, Doktrin und Aktualität eines prophetischen Lehrschreibens.* Cologne: Editiones Una Voce, 2000.

Berthier, Joachim-Joseph. *Sanctus Thomas Aquinas "Doctor Communis" Ecclesiae,* Vol. I: *Testimonia Ecclesiae.* Rome: Typographia Editrice Nazionale, 1914.

Bertuletti, Angelo. *La presenza di Cristo nel Sacramento dell'Eucaristia* (Corona Lateranensis, 19). Rome: Pont. Univ. Lateranense, 1969.

Bonino, Sergé-Thomas, Editor. *Saint Thomas d'Aquin et le Sacerdoce. Actes du colloque organisé par l'Institut Saint-Thomas-d'Aquin les 5 et 6 juin à Toulouse* published as *RT* 99 (1999), no. 1. Toulouse: Ecole de Théologie, 1999.

Brennan, Robert E. *Thomistische Psychologie.* Heidelberg: Kerle, 1957.

Browe, Peter. "Die scholastische Theorie der eucharistischen Verwandlungswunder." *Theologische Quartalschrift* 110 (1929), 305–32.

Cappelli, Tullio. "La significazione sacramentale." *Studi tomistici* 13 (1981): 424–27.

Cessario, Romanus. *Le Thomisme et les Thomistes.* Paris: Cerf, 1999.

Clement, André. *La sagesse de Thomas d'Aquin.* Paris: Nouvelles editions Latines, 1983.

Colosio, I. "La lode divina nel commento ai Salmi di S. Tommaso." *Rassegna di ascetica e mistica* 43 (1975): 179–86.

Darms, Gion. *700 Jahre Thomas von Aquin. Gedanken zu einem Jubiläum.* Freiburg/Switzerland: Paulusverlag, 1974.

Descourtieux, Paul. "Theologie und Liturgie der Eucharistie beim hl. Thomas von Aquin." *Una Voce Korrespondenz* 8 (1978): 18–23.

Diekamp, Franz/Jüssen, Klaudius. *Katholische Dogmatik nach den Grundsätzen des heiligen Thomas,* Vol. III. Münster: Aschendoff, 1954.

Dominicus a Marinis. *Expositio commentaria in tertiam partem Summae Doctoris Angelici Sancti Thomae.* Lyon: Philippi Borde & Laurent Arnaud, 1666.

Dörholt, Bernhard. *Der Predigerorden und seine Theologie. Jubiläumsschrift.* Paderborn: Schöningh, 1917.

Elders, Leo J. *Die Metaphysik des Thomas von Aquin,* Vol. I. Salzburg: Pustet, 1985.

Fernandez, Pedro. "Liturgia y teologia. La historia de un problema metodológico." *CienTom* 99 (1972): 135–79.

Floucat, Yves. *Vocation de l'homme et sagesse chrétienne.* Paris: Editions Saint Paul, 1989.

Fries, Albert. "Die eucharistische Konzelebration in der theologischen Kontroverse des 13. Jahrhunderts." Edited by Franz Groner. *Die Kirche im Wandel der Zeit* (FS Cardinal Höffner). Cologne: Bachem, 1971: 341–52.

———. "Einfluß des Thomas auf liturgisches und homiletisches Schrifttum des 13. Jahrhunderts." Edited by Willehad Paul Eckert. *Thomas von Aquino. Interpretation und Rezeption.* Mainz: Grünewald, 1974: 309–453.

Gaillard, J. "La théologie des mystères." *Revue Thomiste* 57 (1957): 510–51.

Gamber, Klaus. *Fragen in die Zeit.* Regensburg: Pustet, 1989.

Garrigou-Lagrange, Réginald. *Mystik und christliche Vollendung.* Augsburg: Haas und Grabherr, 1927.

———. *Le Sacrifice de la Messe.* Var: Le Sainte-Baume, 1933.

———. *De Deo uno. Commentarium in Primam Partem S. Thomae.* Rome-Paris: Marietti, 1937.

———. *De Eucharistia. Commentarius in Summam theologicam S. Thomae.* Rome-Turin: Marietti, 1946.

————. *De Christo Salvatore. Commentarius in IIIm Partem Summae thelogicae S. Thomae.* Rome–Turin: Marietti, 1946.

————. *La mère de Sauveur.* Paris-Montreal: Cerf, 1948.

————. *La synthèse thomiste.* Paris: Desclée, 1950.

Gherardini, Brunero. "Eucaristica ed ecumenismo," Piolanti, in *Il Mistero,* 651–55.

González Fuente, Antolin. "La theologia nella liturgia e la liturgia nella teologia in san Tommaso d'Aquino." *Angelicum* 74 (1997): 359–417, 551–601.

Grabmann, Martin. *Die Kulturphilosophie des hl. Thomas von Aquin.* Augsburg: Benno Filser, 1925.

————. *Einführung in die Summa theologiae des heiligen Thomas von Aquin.* Freiburg/Breisgau: Herder, 1928.

————. *Introduction to the theological Summa of St. Thomas.* Translated by John S. Zybura. St. Louis: Herder, 1930.

————. *The Interior Life of St. Thomas Aquina.* Translated by Nicholas Ashenbrenner, OP. Milwaukee: Bruce, 1951.

————. *Thomas von Aquin. Persönlichkeit und Gedankenwelt: Eine Einführung.* Munich: Kösel, 1949.

Guardini, Romano. *Vom Geist der Liturgie.* Freiburg/Breisgau: Herder, 1962.

————. *The Spirit of the Liturgy.* Translated by Ada Lane. London, Sheed & Ward, 1937.

Guz, Tadeus. "Der inkarnierte Logos als Ursprung, Wesen und Ziel der hl. Liturgie der Kirche." *Doctor Angelicus* 1 (2001): 201–5.

Gy, Pierre-Marie. "L'Office du Corpus Christi et S. Thomas d'Aquin." *RSPT* 64 (1980) : 491–507.

————. "L'Office du Corpus Christi et la théologie des accidents eucharistiques." *RSPT* 66 (1982): 81–86.

Hanssens, Jean-Michel. "De Natura Liturgiae ad mentem S. Thomae." *PRMCL* 24 (1935): 127–65.

Härdelin, Alf. "Die Liturgie als Abbreviatur der Heilsökonomie." *Atti del Congresso Internazionale: Tommaso d'Aquino nel suo settimo centenario,* Vol. 4, Naples: Ed. Domenicane, 1976: 433–43.

Hoeres, Walter. *Gottesdienst als Gemeinschaftskult—Ideologie und Liturgie.* Bad Honnef: Verlag Johannes Bökmann, 1992.

Holböck, Ferdinand. "Thomas von Aquin als? Doctor Angelicus." *Studi Tomistici* 2 (1977): 199–217.

Hoping, Helmut. *Weisheit als Wissen des Ursprungs. Philosophie und Theologie in der* Summa contra gentiles *des Thomas von Aquin.* Freiburg/Breisgau: Herder, 1997.

Hull, Geoffrey. *The Banished Heart. Origins of Heteropraxis in the Catholic Church.* Richmond: Spes Nova League, 1995.

Jenkins, John I. *Knowledge and Faith in Thomas Aquinas.* Cambridge: Cambridge University Press, 1997.

John Paul II. *Die Schwelle der Hoffnung überschreiten.* Hamburg: Hoffmann & Campe, 1994.

———. *Crossing the Threshold of Hope.* Translated by Jenny and Martha McPhee. New York: Random House, 1994.

———. "Il metodo de la dottrina di san Tommaso in dialogo con la cultura contemporanea." Edited by Antonio Piolanti. *Atti dell'VIII Congresso Tomistico Internazionale,* Vol. I. Vatican: Libreria Editrice Vaticana, 1981, 9–20.

Jungmann, Joseph A. *Missarum Sollemnia.* Vienna: Herder, 1949.

Kindlimann, Hans. "Zu den Beziehungen zwischen dem Sakrament als Gnadenmittel und dem Glauben der es spendenden Kirche. Eine Interpretation und Weiterführung von Anschauungen des Doctor communis." *Doctor Angelicus* 1 (2001): 99–186.

Kleber, Hermann. *Glück als Lebensziel. Untersuchungen zur Philosophie des Glücks bei Thomas von Aquin.* Munster: Aschendorff, 1988.

Koster, Mannes D. *Ekklesiologie im Werden.* Paderborn: Schöningh, 1940.

Kranemann, Benedikt. "Liturgiewissenschaft angesichts der Zeitenwende." Edited by Hubert Wolf. *Die katholisch-theologischen Disziplinen in Deutschland 1870–1962.* Paderborn: Schöningh, 1999: 351–76.

Kunzler, Michael. "La liturgia all'inizio del terzo millennio." Edited by Rino Fisichella. *Il Concilio Vaticano II Recezione e attualità alla luce del Giubileo.* Milan: Ed. San Paolo, 2000: 217–31.

Lais, Hermann. *Die Gnadenlehre des heiligen Thomas in der Summa Contra Gentiles und der Kommentar des Franziskus Sylvestris von Ferrara.* Munich: Karl Zink Verlag, 1951.

Lakebrink, Bernhard. *Hegels dialektische Ontologie und die thomistische Analektik.* Cologne: Bachem, 1955.

———. *Klassische Metaphysik. Eine Auseinandersetzung mit der existentialen Anthropozentrik.* Freiburg: Rombach, 1967.

———. *Die Wahrheit in Bedrängnis.* Stein am Rhein: Christiana, 1986.

———. *Perfectio omnium perfectionum.* Città del Vaticano: Libreria editrice Vaticana, 1984.

Leccisotti, Tommaso. "Il Dottore angelico a Montecassino." *RFNS* 32 (1940): 519–47.

Lécuyer, Joseph. "Réflexions sur la théologie du culte selon saint Thomas," *RT* 55 (1955): 339–62.

Lemmonyer, A. "L'oraison et la liturgie d'après St. Thomas." *Vie spirituelle* 11 (1924): 5–16.

Levering, Matthew. *Christ's Fulfillment of Torah and Temple. Salvation according to Thomas Aquinas.* Notre Dame: Notre Dame University Press, 2002.

Lillers, Jacques de. "La Croix, la messe, la Cène . . . et La Clef de la doctrine eucharistique." *Présence du Christ dans la liturgie. Actes du sixième colloque d'études historiques, théologiques et canoniques sur le rite romain.* Paris: Centre International d'Etudes Liturgiques, 2001: 13–66.

Lohaus, Gerd. *Die Geheimnisse des Lebens Jesu in der Summa theologiae des heiligen Thomas von Aquin.* Freiburg/Breisgau: Herder, 1985.

Lorenzer, Alfred. *Das Konzil der Buchhalter.* Frankfurt/Main: Fischer Taschenbuchverlag, 1984.

Lubac, Henri de. *Corpus mysticum. Kirche und Eucharistie im Mittelalter. Eine historische Studie.* Einsiedeln: Benziger, 1969.

Lucien, Bernard. "Das Opfer nach der 'Summa Theologiae' des heiligen Thomas von Aquin." *Altar und Opfer.* Berlin–Paris: Centre International d'Etudes Liturgiques, 1997, 34–67.

Macrelli, Ciro. "La lode e il canto in San Tommaso d'Aquino." *Studi Tomistici* 13 (1981): 447–53.

Maidl, Lydia. *Desiderii interpres. Genese und Grundstruktur der Gebetstheologie des Thomas von Aquin.* Paderborn: Schöningh, 1994.

Manser, Gallus M. *Das Wesen des Thomismus.* Freiburg, Switzerland: Paulusverlag, 1949.

Marimon, Richard. *De Oratione. Juxta S. Thomae doctrinam.* Rome-Puerto Rico: Herder, 1963.

Masi, Roberto. "La conversione eucaristica nella teologia odierna." *Divinitas* 2 (1966): 272–315.

Mattei, Roberto de. "Überlegungen zur Liturgiereform." *Una Voce Korrespondenz* 32 (2002): 61–77.

May, Georg. "Die Liturgiereform des Zweiten Vatikanischen Konzils." Edited by Hansjakob Becker. *Gottesdienst—Kirche—Gesellschaft.* St. Ottilien: Eosverlag, 1991.

Meegeren, Dominicus van. *De Causalitate instrumentali Humanitatis Christi juxta D. Thomae doctrinam.* Rome: Pontificium Institutum Angelicum, 1939.

Menessier, J. "L'idée du sacré et le culte d'après S. Thomas." *RSPT* 19 (1930): 63–82.

Metz, Johann B. *Christliche Anthropozentrik. Über die Denkform des Thomas von Aquin.* Munich: Kösel, 1962.

Metz, Wilhelm. *Die Architektonik der Summa Theologiae des Thomas von Aquin. Zur Gesamtsicht des Thomanischen Gedankens.* Hamburg: S. Meiner, 1998.

Metzger, Marcel. *Geschichte der Liturgie.* Paderborn: Schöningh, 1998.

Meyer, Hans. *Thomas von Aquin. Sein System und seine geistesgeschichtliche Stellung.* Paderborn: Schöningh, 1961.

Milano, A. "Il Sacerdozio nella Ecclesiologia di S. Tommaso d'Aquino." *Asprenas* 17 (1970): 59–107.

Millet-Gérard, Dominique. *Claudel thomiste?* Paris: Champion, 1999.

Morgott, Franz von Paula. *Der Spender der heiligen Sakramente nach der Lehre des heiligen Thomas von Aquin.* Freiburg/Breisgau: Herder, 1886.

Mosebach, Martin. "Was die klassische römische Liturgie für das Gebet bedeutet." *Pro Missa Tridentina* 9 (1995): 4–25.

Neunheuser, Burkhard. *Eucharistie in Mittelalter und Neuzeit (Handbuch der Dogemengeschichte, Vol. IV/4b).* Freiburg/Breisgau: Herder, 1963.

Nyssen, Wilhelm, Editor. *Simandron—Der Wachklopfer. Gedenkschrift für Klaus Gamber (1919–89).* Cologne: Luthe-Verlag, 1989.

O'Meara, Thomas F. *Thomas Aquinas Theologian.* Notre Dame: University of Notre Dame Press, 1997.

Oppenheim, Philippus. *Principia theologiae liturgicae.* Turin: Marietti, 1947.

Parsch, Pius. *Das Jahr des Heiles,* Vol. III. Klosterneuburg: Verlag Volksliturgisches Apostolat, 1938.

Pesch, Otto-Hermann. *Thomas von Aquin. Grenze und Größe mittelalterlicher Theologie.* Mainz: Grünewald, 1995.

Philippe, Marie-Dominique. *Gott allein. Anbetung und Opfer.* Aschaffenburg: Pattloch, 1959.

Philippus a Ss. Trinitate. *Summa theologiae thomisticae seu Disputationes in omnes partes Summae S. Thomae,* 5 Vol. Lyon: Borde & Arnaud, 1653.

Pieper, Josef. *Über die Schwierigkeit heute zu glauben.* München: Kösel, 1974.

———. *Problems of Modern Faith.* Translated by Jan van Heurck. Chicago: Franciscan Herald Press, 1986.

———. "Über einen verschollenen Vorschlag zum Zweiten Vatikanum." Edited by Walter Baier, et al. *Weisheit Gottes— Weisheit der Welt (Festschrift für Cardinal Ratzinger),* Vol. II. St. Ottilien: Eosverlag, 1987: 971–75.

Piolanti, Antonio. *Il Mistero Eucaristico,* Città del Vaticano: Libreria editrice Vaticana, 1983.

Prümmer, Dominicus, Editor. *Fontes vitae s. Thomae Aquinatis,* Fasc. II. Saint Maximin (Var): Librairie Saint-Thomas-d'Aquin, 1924.

Przywara, Erich. "Thomismus und Molinismus." *Stimmen der Zeit* 58 (1933): 26–35.

Rahner, Karl. *Schriften zur Theologie.* Einsiedeln: Benziger, 1957.

————. *Theological Investigations,* Vol. XIII. Translated by David Bourke. New York: Crossroads, 1975.

————. *Das Geheimnis unseres Christus.* Munich: Ars sacra, 1959.

————. *Grundkurs des Glaubens.* Freiburg/Breisgau: Herder, Sonderausg, 1984.

————. *Foundations of Christian Faith.* Translated by William V. Dych. London: Longmann & Todd, 1978.

Ramirez, Jacobo M. *De auctoritate doctrinali S. Thomae Aquinatis.* Salamanticae: Sanctum Stephanum, 1952.

Ratzinger, Joseph Cardinal. "Eucharistie und Mission." *Forum Katholische Theologie* 14 (1998): 81–98.

Rohrbasser, Anton. *Heilslehre der Kirche. Dokumente von Pius IX bis Pius XII.* Freiburg/Switzerland: Paulusverlag, 1953.

Rückriegel, Helmut. "Papsttum, Gehorsam und der liturgische Traditionsbruch." *Una Voce Korrespondenz* 26 (1996): 391–415.

Sala, Giovanni B. "Transubstantiation oder Transsiginifikation?" *Zeitschrift für Katholische Theologie* 92 (1970): 1–34.

Salerno, Luigi. "S. Tommaso e la Costituzione sulla Liturgia." *Sapienzia* 18 (1965): 264–79.

Scheffczyk, Leo. *Katholische Dogmatik, Vol. I: Grundlagen des Dogmas.* Aachen: MM-Verlag, 1997.

————. "Theologie und Moderne." *Forum Katholische Theologie* 13 (1997): 283–90.

Schenk, Richard. "*Omnis actio nostra est instructio.* The Deeds and Sayings of Jesus as Revelation in the View of Aquinas." *Studi Tomistici* 37 (1990): 104–31.

Schmaus, Michael, Editor. *Aktuelle Fragen zur Eucharistie.* Munich: Max Hueber, 1960.

Schmidbaur, Hans C. *Personarum Trinitas. Die trinitarische Gotteslehre des hl. Thomas von Aquin.* St. Ottilien: Eosverlag, 1995.

Schmitz, Rudolf M. "Inkarnation, Geschichte und Meßopfer." *Una Voce Korrespondenz* 26 (1996): 335–52.

Sedlmayr, P. "Die Lehre des hl. Thomas von den accidentia sine subjecto remanentia." *Divus Thomas* (F) 3–12 (1934): 315–26.

Seidl, Horst. "Zum Substanzbegriff der katholischen Transubstantiationslehre." *Forum Katholische Theologie* 11 (1995): 1–18.

Stickler, Alfons M. Cardinal. "Der Vorrang des Göttlichen in der Liturgie." *Una Voce Korrespondenz* 27 (1997): 323–27.

Stöhr, Johannes. "Die thomistische Theozentrik der Theologie und neuzeitliche Auffassungen." *Studi Tomistici* 13 (1981): 87–107.

Teran, Sisto. *Santo Tomas, Poeta del Santisimo Sacramento.* Buenos Aires: Universidad del Norte, 1979.

Tocco, Wilhelm von. *Das Leben des heiligen Thomas von Aquino. Übersetzt und herausgegeben von Willehad Paul Eckert.* Düsseldorf: Patmos Verlag, 1965.

Torrell, Jean-Pierre. *Magister Thomas. Leben und Werk des Thomas von Aquin.* Freiburg/Breisgau: Herder, 1995.

———. *Saint Thomas Aquinas, Volume 1, The Person and His Work.* Translated by Robert Royal. Washington, D.C.: The Catholic University of America Press, 1996.

———. *Saint Thomas d'Aquin, maître spirituel.* Fribourg: Editions Universitaires, 1996.

Utz, Arthur F. *Religion—Opfer—Gebet—Gelübde.* Paderborn: Schöningh, 1998.

Vaggagini, Cyprian. *Theologie der Liturgie.* Einsiedeln: Benziger, 1959.

Walsh, Liam G. "Liturgy in the Theology of St. Thomas." *Thomist* 38 (1974): 557–83.

———. "The Divine and the Human in St. Thomas' Theology of Sacraments." Edited by C.-J. Pinto de Oliveira. In *Ordo sapientiae et amoris*. Fribourg: Editions Universitaires, 1993, 321–52.

Index

About the Author

David Berger is co-founder and editor-in-chief of the German periodical Doctor Angelicus. A corresponding member of the Pontifical Academy of St. Thomas Aquinas, he has published articles in such journals as *Angelicum*, *Divinitas*, and *Gregorianum*. He is the author of, among other books, *Thomismus* (2001), *Thomas von Aquin begegnen* (2002), and most recently *Thomas von Aquins Summa theologiae* (2004).